Rosemary Manning's book of

RAILWAYS
AND
RAILWAYMEN

Illustrated with prints and photographs

KESTREL BOOKS

Rosemary Manning's book of

RAILWAYS
AND
RAILWAYMEN

KESTREL BOOKS
Published by Penguin Books Ltd,
Harmondsworth, Middlesex, England

Copyright © 1977 by Rosemary Manning

First published 1977

ISBN 0 7226 5351 4

Printed in Great Britain by
Butler & Tanner Ltd,
Frome and London

This book is dedicated to the memory of the Somerset and Dorset Railway, affectionately known to its passengers as 'the slow and dirty'

Contents

Acknowledgements

The publishers and author would like to thank the following for their kind permission to reproduce extracts from copyright material: pp. 98–9 Allen & Unwin Ltd, *Britain's Greatest Rail Disaster* by J. A. B. Hamilton; pp. 88–9, 104–5 Angus & Robertson (UK) Ltd, *The Australian Book of Trains* by J. H. and W. D. Martin; pp. 70–71 Ascherberg, Hopwood & Crew Ltd, *The Muddle-Puddle Porter* written and composed by George Grossmith, Jnr; pp. 43–6, 56–7 excerpted from *Bridges and Men* by Joseph Gies, copyright © 1963 by Joseph Gies, reprinted by permission of Cassell & Collier-Macmillan Publishers Ltd and Doubleday & Company, Inc.; pp. 130–31 'Night Mail', reprinted by permission of Faber & Faber Ltd from *Collected Shorter Poems* by W. H. Auden; pp. 133–7 Guinness Superlatives Ltd, *The Guinness Book of Rail Facts and Feats* by John Marshall; pp. 121–3 George Harrap & Co. Ltd, *The Railway Policemen* by J. R. Whitbread; pp. 37–9 Herbert Jenkins, *The Children of the Dead End* by Patrick McGill, reprinted by permission of Barrie & Jenkins Ltd; pp. 63, 66–7 *Journal of the History Workshop* (Ruskin College, Oxford), 'A Glossary of Railwaymen's Talk' by Frank McKenna; pp. 57–9, 106–7 from *Clear the Track* by Louis Wolfe, copyright © 1952 by Louis Wolfe, reprinted by permission of J. B. Lippincott Company; pp. 23, 53–5 Longman, *Isambard Kingdom Brunel* by L. T. C. Rolt, 1957, copyright © L. T. C. Rolt 1957, reprinted by permission of Penguin Books Ltd; pp. 112–14 McGraw Hill Publications, *Railroad Avenue* by Freeman Hubbard, reprinted by permission of Freeman Hubbard; pp. 128–9 New Science Publications, 'Kelly Rides Again' by Colin MacInnes, which first appeared in *New Society*, London, a weekly review of the social sciences; pp. 126–7, 127–8 The Observer Ltd, article by Roy Perrott 1964 and article in colour magazine 1976, reprinted by permission of Transworld Feature Syndicate; 110–11 Seeley, Service & Co. Ltd, *The Making of the Great Canadian Railway* by F. A. Talbot, reprinted by permission of Leo Cooper Ltd; p. 119 Maurice Temple Smith Ltd, *The Victorian Underworld* by Kellow Chesney.

The author and publishers would like to thank the following for their kind permission to reproduce illustrative material: Australian Information Service, London for p. 134 *above*; Australian War Memorial Photograph p. 105; Reproduced by permission of the *Bath and West Evening Chronicle* pp. 100 and 101; Borough of Thamesdown – Great Western Railway Museum, Swindon, for p. 80; British Library for p. 70 *above*; British Rail, Scotland, for p. 99 *both*; British Railways Board for pp. 11 *left*, 63, 77 and 130; Burlington Northern Inc. for pp. 58 and 59 *above*; Canadian Pacific for p. 109 *all*; Chicago and North Western Transportation Company for pp. 113 *below*, 114 and 115; Photograph Desmond Tripp Studios pp. 24 and 135 *below*; By permission of the Editor of the *Dickensian Magazine* p. 97; Dundee Museums and Art Galleries for p. 47 *above*; Sir John Elliot for p. 31; Still courtesy

Acknowledgements

of EMI Film Distributors Ltd p. 118; From the collection of Freeman Hubbard pp. 116 *both* and 117 *both*; *The Illustrated London News* for pp. 16 *below* and 47 *below*; Iowa State Historical Department, Division of Historical Museum and Archives Division, Des Moines, Iowa, U.S.A., for pp. 111 and 113 *above*; Keystone for pp. 126, 128 and 129; Leicestershire Museums Newton Collection for pp. 35, 38 and 39; London Express News and Feature Services for p. 104 *above*; From *Manner and Customs of ye Englyshe 1849* drawn by Richard Doyle p. 79; Mary Evans Picture Library for pp. 96 and 125; National Library of Australia for pp. 90 *above right* and 104 *below*; Trustees of the National Library of Scotland for p. 40; National Portrait Gallery, London, for p. 23 *middle*; National Railway Museum, York, for pp. 15 *below*, 65 and 136 *above*; Novosti Press Agency for p. 134 *below*; Ed Nowak Penn Central Photo p. 137 *left*; Public Transport Commission of New South Wales for pp. 89 and 90 *above left*; Radio Times Hulton Picture Library for pp. 3, 20, 22, 25, 30, 34 *both*, 48 *both*, 50, 55, 56 *both*, 57 *above*, 67, 68, 76, 72 *all*, 73 *all*, 82 *all*, 83 *both*, 84, 85 *both*, 108 *both*, 120 and 135 *above*; W. Heath Robinson from his book *Railway Ribaldry* published by Duckworth p. 26 *below*; By kind permission of the President and Council of the Royal College of Surgeons of England p. 23 *below*; Roy Mitchell Photography for p. 133; Crown Copyright. Science Museum, London, for pp. 11 *right*, 13 *below right*, 15 *above* and 17; Photos. Science Museum, London, pp. 13 *below left*, 14, 16 *above*, 18 *above*, 19, 21 *all*, 23 *above*, 26 *above*, 27 *both*, 28 *both*, 29 *both*, 32, 33, 44 *both*, 45 *both*, 46 52, 53, 54 *both*, 61 *both* and 137 *right*; Photo. Science Museum, London, by permission of the Smithsonian Institute, Washington, p. 57 *below*; Photo. Science Museum, London, from a water-colour drawing by T. P. Rowlandson p. 13 *above*; Lent to Science Museum, London, by Mr T. Lewis, London, p. 18 *below*; Photo. Société Bertin et Cie p. 136 *below*; VicRail for p. 90 *below both*; The Welbeck Gallery for pp. 70 *below* and 71 *both*; Western Americana Picture Library for pp. 59 *below*, 86 and 87.

Introduction

This is a book about railwaymen. Many of its pages were written by railway workers of all kinds – engineers, guards, drivers, signalmen. The accounts of their lives on the railway are fascinating, but often rather long for our purposes, so I have frequently cut the passages I quote, to give them pace. These cuts are not shown in the text.

There are few technical details in the book, but if you want to find out how the *Rocket* illustrated on the right developed, in 150 years, into the inter-city express in the picture below, the principal facts and feats in railway history are set out at the end of the book, together with a list of books for further reading.

Chapter One

Men of vision

George Stephenson (1781–1848) is often called 'the Father of railways'. This is fair enough provided that we remember he was not the first nor the only man to experiment with a steam-engine on wheels – a locomotive. In the mining areas of Cornwall, south Wales and north-east England engineers were grappling with the problems at the turn of the nineteenth century. The chief difficulty was to produce steam under sufficiently high pressure to make a locomotive powerful enough to pull heavy wagons. Allied with this problem was the search for a rail to take the weight of the engine. The early wooden and cast-iron rails used at mines were of little use. Men like Richard Trevithick, the 'Cornish giant', and Timothy Hackworth and William Hedley in north-east England, were pioneers in the field, and the names of some of their experimental locomotives are part of railway history: the *Catch me who can*, the *Puffing Billy* and *Wylam Dilly*. But the real break-through came

Top: Richard Trevithick's Catch me who can *taking passengers on a pleasure trip in Euston Square, 1809*

A front view of Puffing Billy *and a side view of* Wylam Dilly. *Both locomotives survive and are the earliest full-size locomotives still in existence*

with George Stephenson's engine *Blucher*, which he built at Killingworth Colliery in Northumberland, where he was chief engineman. Its first run was on 25 July 1814. George was then thirty-three years old. Since early boyhood he had worked ceaselessly on any engine he could lay his hands on. His father was a fireman, moving from mine to mine, and George worked in the pits too, driving horses for tuppence a day when he was eight, then picking over coke for stones for sixpence a day until he became, at fourteen, assistant fireman to his father at a shilling a day. He had no schooling until he attended nightschool when he was eighteen, and even then he never learned to read or write fluently, and remained a very bad speller all his life. Nevertheless his long experience with colliery pumping-engines and his own inventiveness made him a first-class

The Stephenson family: George is seated and Robert stands beside him. An early type of colliery locomotive is shown in the background

engineer, and, where earlier men had given up, George Stephenson doggedly pressed on. He saw to it that his son Robert had a really good education, and was immensely proud of the fact that Robert went to Edinburgh University. Robert was to become his father's assistant in the early locomotive experiments, and success was just around the corner nine years after the *Blucher* had made her maiden run in 1814. George wrote to an old friend on 31 March 1823:

DEAR SIR, – From the great elapse of time since I seed you, you will hardly know that such a man is in the land of the living. I fully expected to have seen you about two years ago, as I passed throw Barnsley on my way to south Wales, but being informed you was not at home I did not call. There has been many upes and dowes in this neighbourhood since you left, you would no doubt have heard that Charles Nixon was throughing [thrown] out at Walbottle Collery by his partners. Many of his Familey has turned out verey badley. he has been verey unfortunate in Famaley affairs. I left Walbottle Collery soon also after you and has been verey prosperous in my concerns ever since. I am now concerned as Civil Engineer in different parts of the Kingdom. I have oneley one son who I have brought up in my own profeshion he is now near 20 years of age. I have had him educated in the first Schools and is now at Colledge in Edinbro' I have found a great want of education myself but fortune has made a mends for that want.

I am dear sir yours truly
Geo. Stephenson.

That same year, 1823, Robert left Edinburgh University. Two years later the Stockton and Darlington Railway was opened, built to take

A contemporary advertisement for the Stockton–Darlington line

Locomotion One

Wagons lined up on Brusselton Incline at the opening of the Stockton–Darlington line

coal and other freight from the inland areas of Yorkshire to the coast, to be shipped to London and abroad. The Stephensons had won financial support for the line from a wealthy Quaker wool merchant, Edward Pease, a man who also deserves to be called a 'man of vision', for he devoted his energy to launching this railway, a pioneering venture in transport, against considerable local opposition. George Stephenson was surveyor to the Company, with Robert as one of his assistants.

The engineering works of Robert Stephenson & Company had now been founded, at Newcastle upon Tyne, and here was built for the Darlington line the engine which Robert called *Locomotion One*.

The Stockton to Darlington line was officially opened on Tuesday, 4 October 1825. The *Durham County Advertiser* printed a colourful account of the event. The procession of wagons was

The terminus at Stockton

16

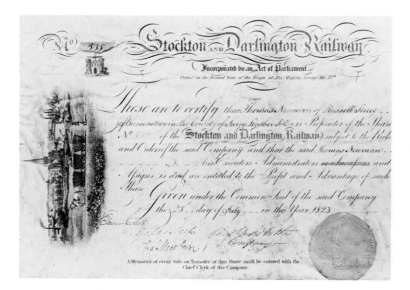

A share certificate of the Stockton and Darlington Railway Company. An Act of Parliament passed in May 1823 allowed the use of locomotives on the line

formed up at Brusselton Incline a few miles beyond Darlington, and hauled on to Stockton by Robert's *Locomotion One.*

The locomotion engine, or steam-horse, as it was more generally termed, gave 'note of preparation' by some heavy aspirations which seemed to excite astonishment and alarm among the 'Johnny Raws', who had been led by curiosity to the spot, and who, when a portion of the steam was let off, fled in a fright, accompanied by the old women and young children who surrounded them, under the idea, we suppose, that some horrible explosion was about to take place. A number of gentlemen, mounted on well-trained hunters, were seen in the fields on both sides of the railway, pressing forward over hedges and ditches, as though they were engaged in a fox chase, yet they could not at this time keep up with the procession.

It reached Darlington at twelve noon. Some wagons were taken off and coals given to the poor. The rest, including two wagons containing a Mr Meynell's 'band of music', went on to Stockton, between fields crowded with spectators. As it reached the Company's wharf at Stockton, a salute of seven guns was fired, and Mr Meynell's band, after playing indefatigably all the way from Darlington, now struck up 'God save the King', which was followed by 'three times three stentorian cheers'. The distance from Brusselton to Stockton was twenty and a half miles.

It was a landmark in the history of railways; but more important in the lives of the Stephensons were two other events: the building of the Liverpool and Manchester Railway, and the Rainhill locomotive trials. Discontented with slow and costly canal transport, businessmen had been planning for years to build a railway track between the two fast-growing mercantile cities – they had at first, of course, considered only horse-drawn wagons, or cable-hauled trucks powered by stationary engines. The success of the Stockton and Darlington line gave impetus to the plans for the Liverpool and Manchester Railway, and to the idea of using on it these new locomotives or 'steam-horses'. George Stephenson was appointed surveyor to the Railway Company. Robert had gone to South America, so George had to face alone the considerable problems of laying the new track, and also some bitter opposition to it from the angry canal owners.

One of Stephenson's bridges – the Moorish Arch at Edge Hill – over the Liverpool and Manchester line. This engraving shows the scene at the opening of the line in 1830

The announcement that appeared in the Liverpool Mercury *in 1829*

TO ENGINEERS AND IRON FOUNDERS.
THE DIRECTORS of the LIVERPOOL and MAN-CHESTER RAILWAY hereby offer a Premium of £500 (over and above the cost price) for a LOCOMOTIVE ENGINE, which shall be a decided improvement on any hitherto constructed, subject to certain stipulations and conditions, a copy of which may be had at the Railway Office, or will be forwarded, as may be directed, on application for the same, if by letter, post paid.
HENRY BOOTH, Treasurer.
Railway Office, Liverpool, April 25, 1829.

Unhappily George's survey was far from accurate. He had relied too much upon assistants, whose measurements were often faulty. His enemies seized upon this and George was dismissed and the Rennie brothers appointed in his place. However, they seem to have done no better and the Company Directors re-appointed George. He worked round the clock to complete his designs, which included sixty-three bridges on the thirty-mile track, a huge tunnel at the Liverpool end, and a long section across a difficult and treacherous bog called Chat Moss, which no other surveyor had considered possible.

Robert returned to England in November 1827 to find his father white-haired and lined in the face, but from now on father and son were partners. They entered their locomotive, the *Rocket*, in a competition for the best engine, which the railway Directors of the new line had announced, and for which was offered £500 as prize money.

When the trials took place at Rainhill, on 6 October 1829, there were five competitors, and thousands of people came to see them. An account of the trials is given in a letter of the time written by a Mr John Dixon to his brother:

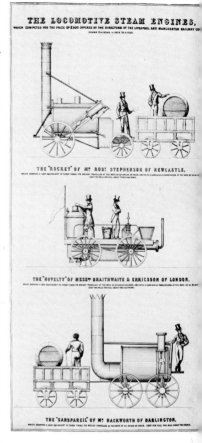

THE LOCOMOTIVE STEAM ENGINES.

THE "ROCKET" OF M.ᵣ ROB.ᵗ STEPHENSON OF NEWCASTLE.

THE "NOVELTY" OF MESS.ʳˢ BRAITHWAITE & ERRICSSON OF LONDON.

THE "SANSPAREIL" OF M.ᵣ HACKWORTH OF DARLINGTON.

Patricroft, Oct. 16 1829

Dear James,

We have finished the grand experiments on the Engines and G.S. or R.S. has come off triumphant and of course will take hold of the £500 so liberally offered by the Company: none of the others being able to come near them. The Rocket is by far the best Engine I have ever seen for Blood and Bone united. Timothy [Hackworth] has been very sadly out of temper ever since he came for he has been grobbing on day and night and nothing our men did for him was right. He got many trials but never got his 70 miles done without stopping. He burns nearly double the quantity of coke that the Rocket does and mumbles and roars and rolls about like an Empty Beer Butt on a rough Pavement and moreover weighs above $4\frac{1}{2}$ Tons. She [Hackworth's engine, the *Sans Pareil*] is very ugly and the Boiler runs out very much, he had to feed her with more Meal and Malt Sprouts than would fatten a pig.

The London Engine of Braithewaite and Erickson called the 'Novelty' was a light one. When she started she seemed to dart away like a Greyhound for a bit but every trial we had some mishap, first an explosion of inflammable gas which burst his Bellows then his feed pipe blew up and finally some internal joint of his hidden flue thro his boiler so that it was no go. Burstall from Edinbro upset his and spent a week in pretending to Remedy the injuries till he was last of all to start and a sorrowful start it was: full 6 miles an hour cranking away like an old Wickerwork pair of Panniers on a cantering Cuddy Ass.

Love to all friends and believe me, Dr [dear] James,

Thy affectionate Bro. in haste,
John Dixon.

Just before the official opening of the Liverpool and Manchester line, parties of sightseers were given rides on it, among them the famous actress, Fanny Kemble, who enjoyed herself hugely, and declared that she was quite in love with George Stephenson, after she had had the thrill of making a journey on the bench of the engine,

The Rocket *comes in first at the Rainhill trials*

with the great man himself at the controls. Here is part of Fanny's letter. You will notice that, like John Dixon, she thinks of the engine as an animal:

We were introduced to the little engine which was to drag us along the rails. She (for they make these curious little fire horses all mares) consisted of a boiler, a stove, a platform, a bench, and behind the bench a barrel containing enough water to prevent her being thirsty for fifteen miles. The reins, bit, and bridle of this wonderful beast, is a small steel handle, which applies or withdraws the steam from its legs or pistons, so that a child might manage it. The coals, which are its oats, were under the bench. This snorting little animal, which I felt rather inclined to pat, was then harnessed to our carriage, and Mr Stephenson having taken me on the bench of the engine with him, we started at about ten miles an hour.

The steam horse being ill adapted for going up and down hill, the road was kept at a certain level, and appeared sometimes to sink below the surface of the earth and sometimes to rise above it.

Almost at starting it was cut through the solid rock which formed a wall on either side of it, about sixty feet high. You can't imagine how strange it was to be journeying on thus, without any visible cause of progress other than the magical machine, with its flying white breath and rhythmical, unvarying pace, between these rocky walls, which are already clothed with moss and ferns and grasses; and when I reflected

20

that these great masses of stone had been cut asunder to allow our passage thus far below the surface of the earth, I felt as if no fairy tale was ever half so wonderful as what I saw. Bridges were thrown from side to side across the top of these cliffs, and the people looking down upon us from them seemed like pygmies standing in the sky.

He (Mr Stephenson) explained to me the whole construction of the steam-engine, and said he could soon make a famous engineer of me, which, considering the wonderful things he has achieved, I dare not say is impossible. His way of explaining himself is peculiar, but very striking, and I understood, without difficulty, all that he said to me. We then rejoined the rest of the party, and the engine having received its supply of water, the carriage was placed behind it, for it cannot turn, and was set off at its utmost speed, 35 miles an hour, swifter than a bird flies (for they tried the experiment with a snipe). You cannot conceive what the sensation of cutting the air was; the motion is as smooth as possible, too. I could either have read or written; and as it was I stood up, and with my bonnet off 'drank the air before me'. The wind, which was strong, or perhaps the force of our own thrusting against it absolutely weighed my eyelids down. When I closed my eyes this sensation of flying was quite delightful, and strange beyond description; yet strange as it was, I had a perfect sense of security, and not the slightest fear.

This pretty little creature can run with equal facility either backwards or forwards, I believe I have given you an account of all her capacities.

Now for a word or two about the master of all these marvels, with whom I am most horribly in love. He is a man from fifty to fifty-five years of age; his face is fine, though careworn, and bears an expression of deep thoughtfulness; his mode of explaining his ideas is peculiar and very original, striking, and forcible; and although his accent indicates strongly his north country birth, his language has not the slightest touch of vulgarity or coarseness. He has certainly turned my head.

George Stephenson

William Huskisson

The day of the opening of the line was cold and squally, but this did not deter the crowds. Unhappily the day began with a fatal accident. William Huskisson, a well-known politician and a Liverpool M.P., was run over by the *Rocket*, and killed. This account of the episode was written by a contemporary writer, Samuel Smiles, ten years after it happened:

The 'Northumbrian' engine, with the carriage containing the Duke of Wellington, was drawn up on one line, in order that the whole of the trains on the other line might pass in review before him and his party. Mr Huskisson had alighted from the carriage, and was standing on the opposite road, along which the 'Rocket' was observed rapidly coming up. At this moment the Duke of Wellington, between whom and Mr Huskisson some coolness had existed, made a sign of recognition, and

The Northumbrian

held out his hand. A hurried but friendly grasp was given; and before it was loosed there was a general cry from the bystanders of 'Get in, get in!'

Flurried and confused, Mr Huskisson endeavoured to get round the open door of the carriage, which projected over the opposite rail; but in so doing he was struck down by the 'Rocket', and falling with his leg doubled across the rail, the limb was instantly crushed. His first words, on being raised, were, 'I have met my death,' which unhappily proved true, for he expired that same evening in the parsonage of Eccles. It was cited at the time as a remarkable fact, that the 'Northumbrian' engine, driven by George Stephenson himself, conveyed the wounded body of the unfortunate gentleman a distance of about 15 miles in 25 minutes, or at the rate of 36 miles an hour. This incredible speed burst upon the world with the effect of a new and unlooked-for phenomenon.

Parkside Station, the scene of Huskisson's death

However, neither the weather, nor Huskisson's death, nor the Iron Duke's unpopularity could spoil the occasion. The first public Railway Company was in operation. A new era had begun.

Almost an exact contemporary of Robert Stephenson was Isambard Kingdom Brunel, both rival and friend of Robert but a man of totally different character. Robert was a solid, hard-working, cautious northcountryman, whose life was dedicated to the production of steam locomotives and railway engineering. Brunel's gifts were very diverse and his character colourful. He experimented

22

in a wide field of engineering and building, including ship design. In his short life – he and Robert Stephenson both died in 1859, only in their fifties – Brunel designed and built most of the Great Western Railway, drove tunnels through the west country hills, constructed some of the most notable aqueducts and bridges in England, designed and launched two iron steam-ships, invented and developed an 'atmospheric' railway (one of his few failures) and left monuments like Paddington Station, Temple Meads Station in Bristol, and the Clifton Suspension Bridge over the Avon, 'my first child, my darling', as he called it.

Brunel was restless, a demon for work, a continual cigar-smoker and a man who looked as if he slept in his clothes, which doubtless did happen at times. He was a brilliantly inventive man who could turn the beam of his imagination not only upon great enterprises, but upon the smallest problem he met with, as is apparent in the domestic upset described by L. T. C. Rolt in this story, which occurred when he was doing conjuring tricks to amuse his children:

It was during one of these nursery entertainments that there occurred the only incident to ruffle seriously the ordered calm of Duke Street. In performing one of his tricks, Brunel accidentally swallowed a half-sovereign which lodged in his wind-pipe and placed him in imminent danger of choking to death. Sir Benjamin Brodie the eminent surgeon was called in and after anxious consultation in which the patient himself joined it was decided to perform a tracheotomy operation using a most horrific instrument nearly two feet long which became known in the profession as 'Brodie's Forceps' although Brunel himself designed it. The operation proved unsuccessful. When the forceps were inserted through the incision in the wind-pipe Brunel found himself unable to breathe and the attempt to locate the coin had to be abandoned, leaving him worse off to the extent of a throat wound. In this serious pass and with the best medical brains of the day defeated, Brunel summoned his own engineering skill to his aid in the form of centrifugal force. He rapidly sketched out a simple piece of apparatus consisting of a board, pivoted between two uprights, upon which he could be strapped down and then swung rapidly head over heels. This was quickly made and the experiment tried while Mary [his wife] and the children's old Irish nurse waited white-faced outside the door of his room. The first trial brought on so violent a fit of coughing and choking that those present feared that his death was imminent and the frame was stopped. But his choking finally subsided and he then signalled them to try once more. As he was swung round he began to cough again and then suddenly felt the coin leave its place. A few seconds later it dropped from his mouth.

Robert Stephenson

Isambard Kingdom Brunel

A pair of forceps similar to those designed by Brunel

23

Brunel's office at 18 Duke Street, London

Brunel's greatest monument is undoubtedly the Great Western Railway, now part of British Rail, of course. In its early nineteenth-century days it was characterized by a startling difference from other railways in Britain, its gauge. The gauge, the width between two lines of rails, used by the Stephensons and other early engineers had been adopted from the width in use for wagons at collieries, that is four feet eight and a half inches. Brunel, appointed Chief Engineer of the G.W.R. when he was only thirty, was autocratic. He rejected what he called the 'coal-wagon' gauge, and persuaded the G.W.R. Directors to adopt a width of *seven* feet, convinced that it would give higher speed with greater safety and stability. The G.W.R. was built with this gauge, but against a barrage of criticism. It made Brunel many enemies and his troubles were increased by inefficiencies among his staff, delays in the delivery of materials, interference from his Directors, and terrible weather. Just before the opening day, 31 May 1838, of the first lap of the G.W.R. he wrote:

If ever I go mad, I shall have the ghost of the opening of the railway walking before me, or rather standing in front of me, holding out its hand, and when it steps forward, a little swarm of devils in the shape of leaky pickle-tanks, uncut timber, half-finished station houses, sinking embankments, broken screws, absent guard plates, unfinished drawings and sketches, will, quietly and quite as a matter of course and as if I ought to have expected it, lift up my ghost and put him a little further off than before.

The railway world was soon divided into two camps over the gauge question. In 1846 matters came to a head, for G.W.R. lines were meeting, at junctions, other railway tracks of the smaller gauge, and this entailed much changing for passengers, not to mention freight. In *Stokers and Pokers* Sir Francis Head gives a vivid picture of the confusion:

At Gloucester it occupied about an hour to remove the contents of a wagon, full of miscellaneous merchandise, from one gauge to another. An ordinary train might contain loose commodities, such as bricks, slates, lime or limestone, and chalk, coal or coke, timber, iron, iron-ore, lead and metals, cast-iron pots, bones and hoofs, potatoes, onions, and other vegetables; cheese, chairs, and furniture; hardware, groceries, provisions, cotton-wool, oils, wines, spirits, and other liquids, manufactured goods, fish and eggs, ripe fruit, etc. In the hurry the bricks are miscounted, the slates chipped at the edges, the cheeses cracked, the ripe fruit and vegetables crushed and spoiled; the chairs, furniture, all more or less broken; the coals turned into slack, and the fish too late for market. Whereas, if there had not been any interruption of gauge, the whole train would, in all probability, have been at its destination long before the transfer of the last article, and without any damage or delay.

No wonder that a Royal Commission declared its opinion that 'the continued existence of the double gauge is a national evil'.

Passengers and luggage being shifted from broad gauge to narrow gauge at Gloucester

Narrow-gauge rails inside broad-gauge rails. This photograph was taken in 1892, the year in which the broad gauge was finally abolished

The changeover from broad to narrow gauge, as seen by one famous illustrator, W. Heath Robinson

The broad gauge was doomed. By the end of the century Brunel's seven-foot gauge from London to Penzance and the rest of the west country had been replaced by the standard four foot eight and a half inches, at huge cost of course. Yet, though Brunel lost the 'battle of the gauges', his claim that he would make the G.W.R. 'the finest work in England' was not unjustified for he left a superbly designed railway, with his genius stamped on every bridge, viaduct and tunnel.

The paths of Brunel and Robert Stephenson crossed hardly at all after their youthful days. It might be thought that Robert was a far more successful man. His locomotives were exported all over the world; he himself travelled widely as a consultant engineer; he was M.P. for Whitby, and lived in London society. Yet no tribute to Robert Stephenson's genius can quite match the heartfelt personal memories of those who had worked under Isambard Kingdom Brunel.

In 1859 Brunel lay paralysed and dying. He kept himself alive almost by an act of will, in order to hear of the success of his last invention, the iron steam-ship *Great Eastern*, then on her maiden trip from Bristol. Instead, the news had to be broken to him that his ship had suffered a tremendous explosion, and was lying crippled at Weymouth. That night Brunel closed his eyes and died.

His lifelong assistant and friend, Daniel Gooch, who had first worked for him in 1837 when he was only twenty, wrote in his diary, when he heard that his old chief had died:

On the 15th September I lost my oldest and best friend. By his death the greatest of England's engineers was lost, the man with the greatest originality of thought and power of execution, bold in his plans but right. The commercial world thought him extravagant; but although he was so, great things are not done by those who sit down and count the cost of every thought and act.

Two of Brunel's most famous achievements are shown opposite. Top: *Maidenhead Bridge.* Below: *Temple Meads Station, Bristol*

26

More of Brunel's achievements are shown on these pages. Above: *Box Tunnel.* Left: *the G.W.R. tunnel near Bristol, drawn on its opening in 1838 by J. C. Bourne.* Above opposite: *Saltash Bridge under construction in 1859.* Below opposite: *Wharncliffe Viaduct at Hanwell*

Buffer: Railways and royalty

We arrived here yesterday morning, having come by railroad from Windsor, in half an hour, free from dust and crowd and heat, and I am quite charmed by it.

Letter from Queen Victoria, 14 June 1842

Mr Isidore, the Queen's coiffeur, who receives £2,000 a year for dressing Her Majesty's hair twice a day, had gone to London in the morning to return to Windsor in time for her toilet; but on arriving at the station he was just five minutes too late, and saw the train depart without him. His horror was great, as he knew that his want of punctuality would deprive him of his place, as no train would start for the next two hours. The only resource was to order a special train, for which he was obliged to pay £18; but the establishment, feeling the importance of his business, ordered extra steam to be put on, and conveyed the anxious hairdresser 18 miles in 18 minutes, which extricated him from all his difficulties.

Thomas Raikes, *Journal 1831–1847*

The royal carriage, with its engine

When the Emperor Nicholas of Russia was asked to decide upon the route of the line between St Petersburg and Moscow he contemptuously tossed aside the plans placed before him, ordered a map to be unrolled on the table, put his sword across the map, and drawing a straight line from one city to the other, regardless alike of rights of way and rights of property, flung his inexorable plan to the astounded surveyor, saying, 'Voilà votre chemin de fer' ['There's your railway'].

John Pendleton, *Our Railways*, 1894

*Louis Philippe of France joins Queen Victoria and Prince Albert in their
private carriage, 1844*

Chapter Two

The bold navvy man

During the nineteenth century, 20,000 miles of railway track were laid from end to end of Great Britain. The men who built it, who drove the tunnels and constructed the cuttings and embankments,

Navvies at work on the construction of a tunnel in 1837

were a huge army of labourers, tough, hard-drinking, mostly illiterate and sometimes lawless. They worked in conditions of incredible hardship, and suffered heavy losses in life and limb. Labour was cheap and little was done by the contractors who hired them to protect their workers from the dangers of slipping embankments, falling tunnels or flooded cuttings. These gangs of workmen came to be known as 'navvies', a name derived from the term 'navigators', which had been used for the men who built the canals in the eighteenth century. The best type of navvy came from the fens of Lincolnshire. These were often skilled men who had built sea-walls, canals and dykes. A rougher, often more desperate, type came from the unemployed farm labourers of Yorkshire and Lancashire, and from Ireland, where the potato famine of 1846 was driving people out in huge numbers to seek a better life in England or the United States. People in Britain complained endlessly of the savagery, godlessness and drunkenness of the navvies, but did nothing to improve their lot. The heavy, dangerous work, and the absence of settled homes, encouraged lawlessness and brutality.

Building a line through solid rock

33

Samuel Smiles gives a detailed description of the navvies in his
Life of George and Robert Stephenson, published in 1862. In
the following account Smiles is writing about the infamous Kilsby
Tunnel on Robert Stephenson's London to Birmingham Railway.
It took five years to build and employed 20,000 men, many of whom
died or suffered terrible injuries.

During the railway-making period, the navvy wandered about from
one public work to another – apparently belonging to no country and
having no home. He usually wore a white felt hat with the brim turned
up, a velveteen or jean square-tailed coat, a scarlet plush waistcoat with
little brown spots, and a bright-coloured kerchief round his herculean
neck, when, as often happened, it was not left entirely bare. His corduroy
breeches were retained in position by a leathern strap round the waist,

*Navvies taking a break
from work on the
Crystal Palace in 1853*

and were tied and buttoned at the knee, displaying beneath a solid calf and foot encased in strong high-laced boots.

Their powers of endurance were extraordinary. In times of emergency they would work for twelve or even sixteen hours, with only short intervals for meals. Reckless alike of their lives as of their earnings, the navvies worked hard and lived hard. For their lodging, a hut of turf would content them; and in their hours of leisure, the meanest public-house would serve for their parlour. The navvies came to be distinguished by a sort of savage manners, which contrasted strangely with those of the surrounding population. Yet, ignorant and violent though they may be, they were usually good-hearted fellows in the main – frank and open-handed with their comrades, and ready to share their last penny with those in distress. Their paynights were often a saturnalia of riot and disorder, dreaded by the inhabitants of the villages along the line of works.

What Samuel Smiles did *not* report was that these men were often cruelly exploited by their employers, nor did he understand that their 'savage manners' were largely the product of brutalizing conditions. He says that they earned good wages, and perhaps by Victorian standards they did. In fact, the *average* wage of a navvy was three shillings a day and few of them received their wages regularly. It was the habit of most contractors to pay them only monthly, sometimes not even as frequently as this. Moreover they usually received their pay packet in a public house, where of course they were tempted to drink away much of it. Another evil was the 'tommy' or 'truck' shop. These were general stores, owned by the employers. Some of the navvies' pay was given in the form of truck tickets which could only be spent in these 'tommy' shops, where prices were far higher than in ordinary stores.

Perhaps the worst aspect of the navvies' lives, and one that was particularly hard for men who worked in dangerous conditions, was the total lack of compensation to those who were injured or crippled, and therefore dismissed. Their families received no compensation either when the breadwinner was hurt or killed. A Select Committee was set up in 1846 to investigate the plight of railway labourers.

Among those who gave evidence to the Committee were two surgeons, Mr J. Roberton and Mr H. L. Pomfret. Mr Roberton had carried out an inspection of the living quarters of the navvies at Woodhead in Cheshire, where a tunnel was under construction. He found them living fourteen and fifteen together in filthy huts, but he was to learn even more serious evidence of the men's sufferings when he met his fellow-surgeon, Mr Pomfret. The latter had been working among the navvies for some time, and told Mr Roberton that so far thirty-two men had been killed in the Woodhead Tunnel, several crippled for life and many wounded by what he called 'less serious injuries', among which he listed fractured skulls and burns from blasting, severe bruises and bone dislocations.

At the Committee's inquiry Mr Pomfret was questioned in person. Here is a short extract from his evidence:

CHAIRMAN: What sort of accommodation was it these men had?
POMFRET: They were huts chiefly built by themselves. I think loose stones and mud, and thatched with ling from the moors.
CHAIRMAN: Have you ever known any cases in which the men had no accommodation for lodging at all?
POMFRET: I have attended several who were hurt that slept in the boiler-houses or stables.
CHAIRMAN: Wounded men?
POMFRET: Wounded men.
CHAIRMAN: Boiler-houses attached to the steam-engine?

It was obvious that the Chairman could hardly believe his ears, but Pomfret confirmed that this was true.

Roberton also gave evidence. One of his most shocking reports concerned a navvy called Lee:

Take the case of a fine, powerful workman who had the spine fractured in such a way as to preclude all hope of recovery. Although this man pleaded again and again to have the scriptures read to him, with religious counsel, the request was in vain; for, after remaining many days in a sinking state, he was allowed to die without having received the least attention from the Church.

At the end of this long and important inquiry the Select Committee recommended that compensation should be paid for injuries and death, but their report was ignored. It was never even debated in Parliament and aroused no public interest or outcry whatever, despite the horrifying conditions that it revealed.

In 1916 an Irish writer called Patrick Macgill published a novel called *Children of the Dead End*. He subtitled it *The Autobiography of a Navvy*. All Macgill's novels deal with the lives and conditions of working men and women. This one tells of a young Irishman who wanders from job to job. The following extract gives a vivid picture of the navvying life and must be based mostly upon his own experiences:

I got a job on the railway and obtained lodgings in a dismal and crooked street, on the south side of Glasgow. The landlady was an Irishwoman, bearded like a man, and the mother of several children. When indoors, she spent most of her time feeding one child, while swearing like a carter at all of the others. We slept in the one room, mother, children and myself, and all through the night the children yelled like cats in the moonshine. The house was alive with vermin. The landlady's husband was a sailor who went out on ships to foreign parts and always returned drunk from his voyages. When at home he remained drunk all the time, and when he left again he was as drunk as he could hold. I had no easy job to put up with him at first, and in the end we quarrelled and fought. He accused me of being too intimate with his wife when he was away from home. I told him that my taste was not so utterly bad, for indeed I had no inclination towards any woman, let alone the hairy and unkempt person who was my landlady. I struck out for him on the stair head. Three flights of stairs led from the door of the house down to the ground floor. I threw the sailor down the last flight bodily and headlong; he threw me down the middle flight. Following the last throw he would not face up again, and I had won the fight. Afterwards the woman came to her husband's aid. She scratched my face with her fingers and tore at my hair, clawing like an angry cat. I did not like to strike her back, so I left her there with her drunken sailor and went out to the streets. Having no money I slept until morning beside a capstan on Glasgow quay. Next day I obtained lodgings in Moran's model, and I stopped there until I went off to London eleven months afterwards.

I did not find much pleasure in the company of my new railway mates. They were a spineless and ignorant crowd of men, who believed in clergycraft, psalm-singing, and hymn-hooting. Not one of them had the pluck to raise his hands in a stand-up fight, or his voice in protest against the conditions under which he laboured. Most of them raised their caps to the overseers who controlled their starved bodies and to the clergy who controlled their starved souls. They had no comprehension of a just God. To them God took on the form of a monstrous and irritable ganger who might be pacified by prayers instead of the usual dole of drink.

I have said before that I am very strong. There was no man on the railway line who could equal me at lifting rails or loading ballast waggons. I had great ambitions to become a wrestler and go on the stage. No workman on the permanent way [i.e. laying down the rails] could rival me in a test of strength.

The shunter of our ballast train was a heavy-shouldered man, and he had a bad temper and an unhappy knack of lifting his fists to those who were afraid of him. He was a strong rung of a man, and he boasted about the number of fights in which he had taken part. He was also a lusty liar and an irrepressible swearer. He felt certain that every man on the permanent way feared him, and maybe that was why he called me an Irish cur one evening. We were shovelling ashes from the ballast waggons on one line into the four-foot way of the other, and the shunter stood on the foot-board of the break-van two truck lengths from me. I threw my shovel down, stepped across the waggons, and taking hold of the fellow by the neck and waist I pulled him over the rim of the vehicle and threw him headlong down the railway slope. I broke his coupling pole over my knee and threw the pieces at his head. The breaking of the coupling pole impressed the man very much. Few can break one over their knees. When the shunter came to the top of the slope again, he was glad to apologize to me.

Once the railway system in Britain was built, the gangs of navvies broke up, with the exception of those men who went on to build docks, reservoirs and such public works. Some navvies had already worked abroad earlier in the century, in France and elsewhere, and now, towards the end of the Victorian Age, hundreds of navvies emigrated for good to Australia, South Africa, India and other countries. But the memory of the 'gangs' lingered on in Britain for many years. They had seemed like a foreign army invading Britain's countryside, often speaking dialects quite unfamiliar and unintelligible to the local shopkeepers and public-house owners where they spent so much of their money. They developed their own slang, which made them even more strange. Much of it was rhyming slang rather similar to that used by London Cockneys. Here is an example, given in Terry Coleman's *Railway Navvies*:

Working on the permanent way

39

'Now, Jack,' says one navvy to another, 'I'm going to get a tiddly wink of a pig's ear, so keep your mince pies on the Billy Gorman' – meaning he is going to get a drink of beer and wants Jack to keep an eye on the foreman.

They must have felt a need for special names, for they were men without roots, far from home, and the nicknames gave them new identities and a sense of belonging together in towns and villages where most men shunned and feared them. Here are a few, taken from Terry Coleman's book:

Punch Any man shorter than usual.
Streaky Dick A man with grey-brown whiskers.
Bacca Lank A Lancashire man who smoked heavily.
Straight-up Gip A thin man.
Starch-em-stiff Another name for a thin man.
Wellington A man with a huge nose, like the Duke of Wellington.
Cat's Meat A reference to a man's old profession.
Mary Ann A man with a high, womanish voice.

Alexander Anderson

As people's memory of the navvies faded, there remained as a permanent memorial to them nearly 20,000 miles of railway track. Yet hardly one of those thousands of navvies has any personal memorial. A Scots navvy, Alexander Anderson, however, achieved some fame as a poet. The following lines, called 'Old Wylie's Stone', commemorate the death of a comrade:

> We stood clear of both lines, and were watching the train
> Coming up with a full head of steam on the strain,
> When all at once one of our men gave a shout –
> There's a shovel against the rail! Look out!
> The shovel was Wylie's, and swift as a wink,
> He sprang into the four feet* with never a shrink;
> Clutched it; but ere he could clear the track,
> The buffer beam hit him right in the back.
> In a moment poor Wylie was over the slope
> And we after him, but with little of hope;
> Found him close by the stone, with his grip firm set
> On the shovel that cost him his life to get.

> *the rails

And one railway company put up a tablet in St Leonard's church at
Chapel-le-Dale, near Ribblehead:

TO THE MEMORY
OF THOSE
WHO THROUGH ACCIDENTS
LOST THEIR LIVES
IN CONSTRUCTING THE
RAILWAY WORKS
BETWEEN SETTLE AND DENT HEAD
THIS TABLET WAS ERECTED
AT THE JOINT EXPENSE
OF THEIR FELLOW WORKMEN
AND THE
MIDLAND RAILWAY COMPANY
1869 TO 1876

Buffer: Working on the line

I am a navvy bold, that's tramped the country round, sir,
To get a job of work, where any can be found, sir.
I left my native home, my friends and my relations,
To ramble up and down and work in various stations.

Chorus

I'm a navvy, don't you see, I'm a navvy in my prime;
I'm a nipper, I'm a tipper, and I'm working on the line.

I left my native home on the first day of September,
That memorable day I still do remember.
I bundled up my kit, Sunday smock and cap put on, sir,
And wherever I do go, folks call me happy Jack, sir.

I've got a job of work in the lovely town of Bury,
And working on the line is a thing that makes me merry.
I can use my pick and spade, likewise my old wheelbarrow;
I can court the lasses, too, but don't intend to marry.

I worked a fortnight there, and then it come to pay-day,
And when I got my wages, I thought I'd have a play-day.
And then a little spree in High Street went quite handy.
Then I set me down in Jenkinson's beside a Fanny Brandy.

I called for a pint of beer, and bid the old wench drink, sir,
But whilst she was a-drinking, she too at me did wink, sir.
Well, then we had some talk; in the back we had a rally;
Then jumped o'er brush and steel, and agreed we'd both live tally.

They called for liquors freely, the jug went quickly round, sir,
That being my wedding day, I spent full many a crown, sir.
And when my brass was done, old Fanny went a-cadging,
And to finish up my spree, I went and sloped my lodgings.

Oh now I'm going to leave the lovely town of Bury;
I'm sorry for to leave you chaps, for I always found you merry.
So call for liquors freely, and drink away my dandy,
Here's a health to happy Jack, likewise to Fanny Brandy.

Chapter Three

Tunnels and bridges

Throughout the nineteenth century Britain led the world in bridge-building. Bridges symbolized the confidence and adventurousness of the Victorian age. They were built to carry the new railway systems over rivers, highways and deep valleys. In the thirty years between 1830 and 1860, the heyday of railway-building, no less than 25,000 railway bridges were constructed. Telford, Brunel, the Stephensons and Rennie are among the greatest names in this field, and all were pioneers in their bold experiments with different types of construction and different materials. Technical advances were eagerly adopted, exploited and improved – heavy mechanical pile-drivers, for instance, and steam traction for hauling and lifting. But the Victorian engineers had to rely first and foremost upon their own wits, for there were few precedents to guide them. George Stephenson supervised personally the building of sixty-three bridges on the thirty miles of his Liverpool and Manchester Railway. He had no trained staff to help him, and every drawing came from his own hand. One of his most important innovations was the use of cast-iron girders to carry the track, thus doing away with the need for conventional arches.

His son Robert was even more adventurous. In the Britannia Bridge over the Menai Straits in north Wales he produced a masterpiece. In *Bridges and Men* Joseph Gies describes the problems that faced Robert in designing this bridge and how he solved them.

Thinking in terms of rigidity, Robert Stephenson tried to picture an iron span that would be strong enough to support a locomotive's weight. Over hundreds of British streams, canals, gulleys and city streets, his father had built short bridges supported by cast-iron beams stretching

A drawing of one of Stephenson's iron tubes under construction

The scene at the Menai Straits in May 1849. The central tower is almost complete

across the full span. Robert Stephenson imagined an enormous iron beam, that could reach out across the Menai Strait. Of course, such a massive iron bar could not be cast, and would take a million or so tons of iron . . .

But suppose the beam were hollow? Suppose one built a succession of rectangular iron boxes open at both ends, riveted together end to end, *through* which trains could run? Certainly the result would be an exceptionally firm span, one that might cross even the Menai Strait. Bracing could be supplied by an intermediate pier on Britannia Rock in the middle of the strait. Stephenson began to picture a complex of four rectangular iron tubes, arranged in two pairs meeting over Britannia Rock.

But would such a structure really withstand the loading of steam trains? Stephenson doubted it, even if it were braced further with chains.

In his dilemma, Robert Stephenson turned to his father. Old Geordie was now enjoying retirement, entertaining friends at what he called 'crowdie nights', not from the crowd of people present, but from a Newcastle oatmeal concoction with which he regaled them. One of his regular visitors was William Fairbairn, an engineer and even a scientist of distinction. Old Geordie considered Robert's tubular-bridge idea and thought it good; Fairbairn suggested experimenting with wrought-iron sheets to ascertain the strength of various weights and forms. Robert Stephenson readily agreed, and in the next few months of 1845 Fairbairn carried out a series of tests.

Stephenson had Fairbairn's conclusions checked and retested, and then determined to plunge ahead. 'I stood on the verge of a responsibility from which I confess I had nearly shrunk,' he wrote later.

The construction of the tubes at the water's edge

Iron plates were brought by ship from Liverpool, Anglesey marble from Penmon on the island, and red sandstone from Cheshire. Fifteen hundred men were soon at work on the mainland, on the Anglesey shore, on Britannia Island, and on boats and barges in the waterways. The central tower, 'Great Britannia', rose 230 feet high on the rocky isle in the strait. The two shore towers were a little shorter.

The work at Menai was pushed; in June 1849 the first of the four tubes was ready to be lifted. At low tide it was hauled to the water's edge. As the tide came in, the big square tube, closed at both ends, was gradually set afloat. Tugs pushed and pulled it into its designated

The second tube is floated into position, ready for hauling up, in December 1849. The first tube can be seen already slotted into place between the two towers

*The finished bridge,
with its four hollow
tubes and three upright
towers*

position. Robert Stephenson mounted the top of the iron monster and
gave hand signals to Captain Claxton, in charge of a corps of sailors
manning the pontoon boats. A sailor in each boat held a distinguishing
letter aloft. Captain Claxton, armed with a speaking trumpet, bellowed
Stephenson's instructions to each capstan by letter. The men turned
the capstans, the hydraulic presses on top of the towers strained, the
heavy chains attached to the tube creaked, and the mass began to lift.
Thousands of spectators lined both shores. But at the outset a capstan
gave way, and the work was postponed to the next morning. After a
day of repair, preparation, and pulling, the great tube was out of the
water by evening. At this critical moment another capstan broke, the
men working it were knocked down by the crazily spinning arm, and
some of them were hurled into the water. Charles Rolfe, in charge of
the broken capstan, shouted for help. The end of the line was paid out
into the crowd on shore; men, women, and children laid hold, and the
tube's fall was checked. By midnight the pontoons were clear and the
mighty tube hung suspended between Britannia Rock and Anglesey, its
end resting on ledges cut in the rocky abutments. The calculations had
been precise; only three quarters of an inch of room was left on either
ledge.

Next morning the labor of raising the tube to its place a hundred
feet above the channel began.

On March 5, 1850, Robert Stephenson drove home the last of the two
million rivets that held the vast cylinders together (that rivet is painted
white to this day), and a short while later rode through the completed
bridge at the head of a train of three locomotives pulling a thousand
persons.

46

Something of what Robert Stephenson went through while building this stupendous bridge comes out in a letter he wrote to a friend:

It was a most anxious and harassing time for me. Often at night I would lie tossing about, seeking sleep in vain. The tubes filled my head. I went to bed with them and got up with them.

Some forty years later, an immensely long bridge was constructed to span the mouth of the river Tay in East Scotland, so that trains could travel directly from the north bank of the Firth of Forth over the Tay mouth to Dundee. The deep inlets of the Forth and Tay had hitherto made a long detour necessary for travellers going from Edinburgh to Dundee. The only way to avoid the detour was to take the even worse trip by ferryboat across the rivers. Now the North British Railway Company planned to bridge the Tay, and later the Forth, so that travellers would have a direct route from Edinburgh to Dundee.

Sir Thomas Bouch

The engineer chosen to build the Tay Bridge was Thomas Bouch, who, it turned out later, had neither the genius of Robert Stephenson nor his infinite capacity for testing every detail personally. When the work started, he was using brick for the piers on the river bed, but he discovered that the borings taken had been inaccurate, and that the bed of the river was not as solid as he had believed. The rest of the piers were built of masonry and onto each were bolted six cast-iron columns filled with concrete. Upon these a lattice-work of iron girders rose above the river. To give headroom to shipping, the girders at the centre were built much higher, with the rails running *within* them instead of on top.

This central portion was referred to as 'the high girders'. When completed in 1878, the Tay Bridge was the longest in the world.

It was inspected and passed as safe, but the inspector issued two qualifications to his approval. He recommended a speed limit of twenty-five m.p.h. and stated that he would like to observe the effect of a high wind on trains crossing the bridge. The inspector's important statements were ignored. Soon after the bridge was opened in May 1878, Queen Victoria travelled across this engineering wonder, to a salute of guns, and knighted the designer, Thomas Bouch, an honour which had not been accorded to either of the Stephensons. The bridge, acclaimed as an engineering masterpiece, was in fact jerry-built, and ended in disaster only eighteen months later.

A view along the inside of the high girders

A contemporary illustration of the Queen's crossing

On the last Sunday of 1879, a fierce gale was blowing up the Firth of Forth, and passengers had a horrible trip in the ferryboat across the river Forth. Having reached the north bank, they must have boarded their Tay Bridge train with considerable relief. The fury of the storm increased. At moments it rose to eighty m.p.h. and by seven o'clock, when the train reached the station at St Fort at the approach to the Tay Bridge, it was difficult for a man to stand up. Signalman Barclay came out of his cabin to attend to a routine job and found himself forced to crawl on all fours.

However, he sent the signal: 'TRAIN ENTERING SECTION' to his fellow-signalman on the north shore of the river. Then he and a surface worker called John Watt watched the tail lights of the train dwindle to pin points as it crossed the bridge. Both of them noticed something odd: sparks flying from the wheels. They had noticed the same phenomenon on the previous train and no satisfactory explanation of this was ever found. Suddenly a violent gust of wind shook the signal cabin. Both men saw a 'sudden brilliant flash of light followed by total darkness'. Tail lights and sparks vanished abruptly. Signalman Barclay found that his instrument was dead and he and Watt set out across the bridge on foot, sensing that something might be amiss, but they were driven back by the wind. They then went down to the shore of the river and, as the moon broke through a heavy cloud for an instant, they saw to their horror that some of the high girders of the bridge had disappeared. Of the train there was no sign at all.

A sailor on a training ship, *Mars*, moored close to the high girders of the bridge, saw the gap as well, and several people on the north shore could see that part of the structure had disappeared, but no one had seen the train. Each side thought that it must have either got over already, or turned back to the south, to St Fort. But hopes faded when mail bags were washed ashore, and pieces of a carriage. At last the truth dawned on those who watched on each side. The gale had blown down a stretch of the bridge – in fact, thirteen of the iron spans, leaving a gap 3,000 feet wide, through which the train must have plunged into the savage river. There could be no survivors.

The only fortunate thing about this sorry affair was that the train was carrying no more than seventy-five passengers that night. Divers later proved that the train had *not* in fact fallen through the gap. Both the train and the high girders through which it was passing had collapsed simultaneously into the waters below, unable to with-

*Steam launches and a
divers' barge are
employed in the fruitless
search for survivors*

stand the pressure exercised by the gale on the flat surface of the
engine and carriages. It was precisely this point that had so worried
the inspector.

Sir Thomas Bouch had to face an inquiry, during which it came
out that the bracing ties of the bridge were not strong enough to
withstand a cross-wind. Out of over 10,000 tons of metal on the
bridge, a high proportion was totally inadequate for the purpose.
Ties had worked loose and the train was thought to have been
travelling too fast, beyond the twenty-five miles an hour recommended by the inspector. The bridge was not flat, and trains
descending the steep gradient at the northern end habitually went
so fast that passengers had been seriously frightened on previous
journeys. Their terror as the high winds battered their coaches on
this trip can only be imagined.

To the ruin and disgrace of the engineer, Bouch, the final
verdict of the inquiry was: 'We find that the bridge was badly
designed, badly constructed and badly maintained.'

Four months later Sir Thomas Bouch died, a broken man.

The Tay Bridge, one of the worst bridges ever built, was im-
mortalized by one of Britain's worst poets, William MacGonagle.
Born in 1830, MacGonagle worked as a weaver and wrote poetry
in his spare time. He called himself 'Sir William Topaz M'Gonagall,
Knight of the White Elephant, Burmah', and celebrated in his
verses every national disaster, adding effusive poetic tributes to

royal and other notable persons. He had already written a glowing account of the Tay Bridge, and when it collapsed he at once turned his talent to the calamity. His poem is well known for its awfulness and is the most famous of his volume entitled *Poetic Gems*.

The Tay Bridge Disaster

Beautiful Railway Bridge of the Silv'ry Tay!
Alas! I am very sorry to say
That ninety lives have been taken away
On the last Sabbath day of 1879,
Which will be remember'd for a very long time.

'Twas about seven o'clock at night,
And the wind it blew with all its might,
And the rain came pouring down,
And the dark clouds seem'd to frown,
And the Demon of the air seem'd to say –
'I'll blow down the Bridge of Tay.'

When the train left Edinburgh
The passengers' hearts were light and felt no sorrow,
But Boreas blew a terrific gale,
Which made their hearts for to Quail,
And many of the passengers with fear did say –
'I hope God will send us safe across the Bridge of Tay.'

But when the train came near to Wormit Bay,
Boreas he did loud and angry bray,
And shook the central girders of the Bridge of Tay
On the last Sabbath Day of 1879,
Which will be remember'd for a very long time.

So the train sped on with all its might,
And Bonnie Dundee soon hove in sight,
And the passengers' hearts felt light,
Thinking they would enjoy themselves on the New Year,
With their friends at home they Lov'd most dear,
And wish them all a happy New Year.

So the train mov'd slowly along the Bridge of Tay,
Until it was about midway,
Then the central girders with a crash gave way,
And down went the train and passengers into the Tay!
The Storm Fiend did loudly bray,
Because ninety lives had been taken away,
On the last Sabbath Day of 1879,
Which will be remember'd for a very long time.

As soon as the catastrophy came to be known
The alarm from mouth to mouth was blown,
And the cry rang out all o'er the town,
Good Heavens! the Tay Bridge is blown down,
And a passenger train from Edinburgh,
Which fill'd all the people's hearts with sorrow,
And made them for to turn pale,
Because none of the passengers were sav'd to tell the tale,
How the disaster happen'd on the last Sabbath Day of 1879
Which will be remember'd for a very long time.

It must have been an awful sight,
To witness in the dusky moonlight,
While the Storm Fiend did laugh, and angry did bray,
Along the Railway Bridge of the Silv'ry Tay,
I must now conclude my lay
By telling the world fearlessly without the least dismay,
That your central girders would not have given way,
At least many sensible men do say,
Had they been supported on each side with buttresses,
At least many sensible men confesses,
For the stronger we our houses do build,
The less chance we have of being killed.

Marc Isambard Brunel

Tunnels do not have quite the glamour of bridges. They rarely inspire romantic feelings in the traveller, who is seldom able to see their often magnificent portals and is only aware of the tunnel when darkness suddenly engulfs the train. The earliest railway tunnels provoked some hysterical opposition. The Victorian railway writer, John Francis, gives an amusing account of it:

The public could not or would not understand that it was as safe to travel in a dark tunnel as on a dark night. It was said that the chill of a two miles subterranean passage would deter any person of delicate health from ever entering them. Sir Anthony Carlisle asserted that 'Tunnels would expose healthy people to cold, catarrhs, and consumption'.

Other doomsters declared that the passengers would be burned alive in their carriages.

There is nonetheless a touch of romance about the tunnel under the Thames built by the Brunels, father and son, perhaps because the younger Brunel was such a colourful figure. His father, Marc, was the engineer for this underwater tunnel running from Rotherhithe to Wapping. He devised shields of metal under which the workmen could dig out the soil, foot by foot. When the section was adequately shored up, the shields were moved forward to a new position. His son, Isambard Kingdom Brunel, then only twenty, took over much of the work. L. T. C. Rolt describes it thus:

And what an amazing drama it was, this stubborn struggle between man and earth which went on relentlessly, month after month, year after year in the darkness under the Thames. Always dramatic, and sometimes tragic, upon one occasion it became sheer fantasy. Isambard Brunel threw into the work all that unsparing energy which was to distinguish his whole life. For as much as thirty-six hours at a time he would not leave the tunnel, pausing only for a brief cat-nap on the wooden stage behind the shield.

As the great shield crept slowly under the river, so the wonder grew, and when 300 ft of the western arch had been completed the directors of the tunnel company began to recoup their fortunes by admitting sightseers at a shilling a head. A barrier was erected to prevent them approaching the shield and here they gathered in awestruck crowds to peer through the gloom at the men who toiled in the gas-lit tiers of the frames. To Marc these visitors were an added anxiety and he protested in vain against their admission. For, with that foresight which was almost prevision, both father and son had measured the appalling risk they were running

One of the metal shields used in the construction of the Thames Tunnel

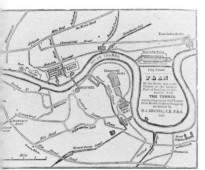

*This map showing the
location of the tunnel
appeared on a
contemporary poster
inviting the public to
view the tunnel 'upon
payment of one shilling
each person'*

*A contemporary
diagram explaining the
position of the tunnel
under the river. At its
furthest point can be
seen the shields in which
the excavators worked*

and guessed that disaster was imminent. Instead of the continuous bed of clay which they had been so confidently promised, they had encountered faults where only gravel separated them from the waters of the river. 'During the preceding night,' wrote Marc Brunel in his diary on 13 May 1827, 'the whole of the ground over our heads must have been in movement, and that, too, at high water. The shield must, therefore, have supported upwards of six hundred tons! It has walked many weeks with that weight, twice a day, over its head! Notwithstanding every prudence on our part a disaster may still occur. May it not be when the arch is full of visitors!'

The debris which fell through into the workings from the bed of the river – pieces of bone and china, an old shoe buckle and finally the sheaf of a block and a shovel – left no doubt as to the state of the ground above. Everything depended on the shield which alone prevented immediate collapse and the movement of a frame became a most hazardous operation.

High water in the river was always the time of danger and on the evening of the 18th as the tide was making, Beamish, who had relieved Isambard Brunel at the frames, put on his waterproof, sou'wester and mud boots in the expectation of a wet night. The tide was making fast and more and more water poured through the shield. Suddenly Beamish heard Goodwin, one of the best of the picked corps of miners who manned the frames, cry out for help. Beamish at once called for assistance from the men in the next frame, but before they had time to reach Goodwin a tremendous torrent of water roared like a mill sluice out of No. 11, bowling over a bricklayer named William Corps who would have been swept off the stage behind the frame had not Beamish managed to cling

to him. Beamish wanted to make a final attempt to enter No. 11 frame but it was impossible. Rogers, one of the men from No. 9, caught his arm, shouting above the thunder of the water: 'Come away, sir, come away; 'tis no use, water's rising fast.' At the visitors' barrier he encountered Brunel and both men turned for a last look at the shield. 'The effect', wrote Beamish afterwards, 'was splendid beyond description; the water as it rose became more and more vivid from the reflected lights of the gas.' Then a great wave advanced down the tunnel carrying with it a chaos of empty cement barrels, boxes and timber spars. It struck a small office building which had been erected midway between the shield and the shaft; there was a deafening crash, and a blast of air as the building collapsed and then all the lights went out. Someone shouted 'The staircase will blow up', and Brunel's voice could be heard ordering the men to ascend the shaft as quickly as possible. Scarcely had the last man cleared it then the lowest flight of the spiral stairway in the shaft was swept away. No sooner had the soaked and exhausted group gained the surface than a faint cry for help was heard from below. The voice was recognized as that of Tillett, the old engineman who had gone below to repack his pumps. Without an instant's hesitation Brunel called for a rope, seized it and slid down one of the iron ties of the shaft into the tumultuous darkness. Miraculously, he managed to find the old man and to secure the rope round his waist as he struggled in the water. When both had been hauled safely up the shaft a roll-call was held. Not a man was missing.

The scene in the tunnel when water began to pour through

It should be added that the tunnel was originally built for carriages and pedestrians. It was long after Brunel's death that it was taken over as a railway tunnel. Today it carries London's underground trains below the Thames.

By the end of the century the tunnel had been taken over by the railway

The pioneering work of the early British engineers in bridge and tunnel construction was soon to be matched by the invention and imaginative scope of foreign engineers. One of the earliest was John Roebling, who bridged the Niagara Falls by a single span of 821 feet, and evoked from Robert Stephenson the generous words: 'If your bridge succeeds, then mine have been magnificent blunders.' The story of the bridge is told in Joseph Gies's *Bridges and Men*.

John Roebling

On March 6, 1855, in defiance of cholera, storm, and the inscrutable treachery of suspension bridges, the Niagara Bridge carried the first train in history to cross a span sustained by wire cables. The inaugural load was a formidable three hundred and sixty-eight tons – a locomotive plus a string of double-loaded cars. In his final report to the bridge company, Roebling set forth a blunt truth in trenchant language.

Professional and public opinion, he noted, had been adverse to suspension bridges for railroads. The Niagara Bridge sustained railroad loading with the aid of 'Weight, Girders, Trusses and Stays. With these any degree of stiffness can be insured, to resist either the action of trains, or the violence of storms, or even hurricanes. And I will here observe, that no Suspension Bridge is safe without some of these appliances. The

Above: *A view along the Niagara Bridge in 1860*

Left: *The complete span of the bridge – over 820 feet*

catalogue of disastrous failures is now large enough to warn against light fabrics, suspended to be blown down. A number of such fairy creations are still hovering about the country, only waiting for a rough blow to be demolished.'

Roebling's words were truly prophetic if we remember the fate of the Tay Bridge in 1879.

Equally dramatic, if less well known, was the construction of a two-mile-long tunnel for the Northern Pacific Railroad in the United States in 1886. Its builder, Nelson Bennett, was not a trained and experienced engineer like Roebling, but an obscure 'roughneck' who had done some oil-prospecting and railroad work out west. Despite the scepticism of some of the N.P.R. Directors, Bennett was appointed to build the tunnel and signed an agreement to complete it in twenty-eight months or forfeit 200,000 dollars. In the face of incredible ill-luck and occasional near-disaster, Bennett carried out the job on time. Louis Wolfe tells the story in *Clear the Track*:

The very day the contract was signed, he made his brother, Captain Sidney Bennett, superintendent. Then the two men decided on what equipment and machinery was needed and ordered it *rush*.

Within a few days the stuff started to pour into Yakima, the end of the railroad tracks – eight boilers, four miles of pipe and two complete saw-mill outfits. Besides that, there were exhaust fans, air compressors, two locomotives and 60 dump cars, arc-light outfits, air drills, several tons of steel drills, several miles of rail and tons and tons of food.

One teamster surveyed the piles of stuff, glanced at Bennett and joked, 'It would be easier to fetch the mountain down here than to fetch all that stuff up there.'

And he was not far from right. From Yakima to the east portal of the tunnel was 82 miles, to the west portal 87. And what miles! There was nothing but raw wilderness – no roads, no bridges and very few trails. The route climbed from 500 feet to 3,000 feet.

Like a general preparing to invade an enemy country, Bennett planned the gigantic task with great care, step by step. First, an overland road had to be laid from the end of the track to where the tunnel would be cut. To build that road he sent an advance guard of seventy-five men out from Yakima. Once the workers reached the two ends of the tunnel site, they had orders to set up stables for the horses, lodging houses for the laborers as well as complete saw-mills, machine shops, etc.

The job of getting the equipment to Stampede Pass was mighty tough. No sooner had the heavily loaded wagons rolled out of Yakima than they sank axle-deep in mud and could not be budged. Horses slipped and fell or collapsed from exhaustion. Instead of making twelve miles a day, wagons rolled only five or four – or even one mile a day! Some were so deeply bogged down in the mud that they had to be abandoned with the machinery.

Back in Yakima, Nelson Bennett paced the floor. 'We've got to get that stuff moving,' he barked. He ordered his men to make a road of wood. A few days later a plank road snaked up the winding foothills. The long wagon train was making pretty good headway until they struck another snag – snow-covered canyons. Bennett ordered his lumberjacks to chop down trees and make sleds out of them. Tons of heavy machinery and supplies were transferred to sleds and lugged up towards Stampede Pass.

Days, weeks, months passed. The mountain was a horror of biting wind. Snow and slush tortured both men and beasts. Day by day the morale of the workers sank lower and lower. They griped, they grumbled, they got into fist fights. It became more and more difficult for Bennett to keep his rough crew on the job. He pleaded, he argued, he threatened. Once the men went on strike and the sheriff had to be called to put down a riot. Several workers were hurt and one killed. Finally, one crew did get to the east portal. Roaring down over the very spot where it was to be dug was a waterfall 170 feet high. Now what?

Nelson Bennett promptly led a crew to the top of the waterfall, then ordered them to make a dam. Within a few days the swift-flowing river was running in another direction! 'Nothing can stop that man,' a blacksmith drawled. 'Just nothing.' Now they were ready to start digging. Until the air drills were brought up, the drilling at both portals was done by hand. And painfully slow it was. Bennett came up with two smart ideas to get the men to work harder. First he offered them a bonus for every

Nelson Bennett

The hospital at Stampede Pass. Accidents were frequent during the building of the tunnel

day they drilled over thirteen and a half feet. Then he got the two crews at the opposite ends of the tunnel to compete against each other. Bennett's stunts worked better than he expected and the crews forged ahead. He worked miracles with men, beasts and machines. But, when it came to the weather, he was as helpless as any man. From March to June of 1886 it snowed day after day and the workers had to drop their tools and shovel the roads clear so the supplies could keep moving up. In the spring and summer of 1887 the rains pelted the men and horses, washed out roads and spoiled tons of food.

On top of all that Bennett was haunted by accidents. Men working at top speed for bonuses worked carelessly. Dynamite blasts were set off too soon or too late, killing and injuring drillers and mechanics. The roof of the tunnel caved in and falling rocks crushed several roustabouts. A landslide killed two teamsters and injured seven others. The Bennett brothers were forced to stay on the job almost twenty-four hours a day. Nelson, especially, was everywhere. When the men went on strike, he was there to break it up. When there were floods, or landslides, or storms he was right on the job. His drive, his iron will, his enthusiasm for the job caught on.

Early in May of 1888 the two crews drilling in the tunnel were so near that they could hear each other. And on May 14 they met! The boring was so exact that they were no more than an inch out of the way. The gigantic task was finished – *only seven days short* of the twenty-eight months!

At work on boring the tunnel. The West's first electric power plant was built expressly to provide light for the construction

Buffer: The Camden Town Cutting

The London–Birmingham railway line was begun in 1834 and the first train left Euston, London's first terminal station, in 1838. In *Dombey and Son* Charles Dickens described the building operations that demolished many houses in Camden Town:

The first shock of a great earthquake had, just at that period, rent the whole neighbourhood to its centre. Traces of its course were visible on every side. Houses were knocked down; streets broken through and stopped; deep pits and trenches dug in the ground; enormous heaps of earth and clay thrown up; buildings that were undermined and shaking, propped by great beams of wood. Here, a chaos of carts, overthrown and jumbled together, lay topsy-turvy at the bottom of a steep unnatural hill; there, confused treasures of iron soaked and rusted in something that had accidentally become a pond. Everywhere were bridges that led nowhere; thoroughfares that were wholly impassable; Babel towers of chimneys, wanting half their height; temporary wooden houses and enclosures, in the most unlikely situations; carcases of ragged tenements, and fragments of unfinished walls and arches, and piles of scaffolding, and wildernesses of bricks, and giant forms of cranes, and tripods straddling above nothing. There were a hundred thousand shapes and substances of incompleteness, wildly mingled out of their places, upside down, burrowing in the earth, aspiring in the air, mouldering in the water, and unintelligible as any dream. Hot springs and fiery eruptions, the usual attendants upon earthquakes, lent their contributions of confusion to the scene. Boiling water hissed and heaved within dilapidated walls; whence, also, the glare and roar of flames came issuing forth; and mounds of ashes blocked up rights of way, and wholly changed the law and custom of the neighbourhood.

In short, the yet unfinished and unopened Railroad was in progress.

Top: *building the retaining wall, September 1836*
Below: *building the engine shed, April 1837*

Chapter Four

The railwaymen

One thing which sets railwaymen apart from other workers is night work. Much of the railwayman's work is done when other people are asleep. One can live in a street with a shift-working railwayman and never realize that he is there, so strange are the hours he keeps.

The hours from midnight until 5 o'clock in the morning are the great time for goods traffic, for the carriage of mail and newspapers, and for the movement of the railway parcel traffic generally. This is the railway that very few people see, when the freight trains are running through the length and breadth of the British Isles, some of them at very great speeds. There are 'Bogie Bolsters' carrying plate and ingots to the big steel works in places like Middlesbrough and Sheffield; 'Piggy-back' trains of half-finished car and lorry frames; oil tankers coming from the Fawley refinery at Southampton; 'Monster' tanks of hydro-chloric acid from the I.C.I. works at Billingham. A lot of food is carried at night. There are the 'Grain Hoppers' which carry grain from the great ports; banana vans; box vans of chocolate; train loads of refrigerated fish and meat.

This quotation comes from *A Glossary of Railwaymen's Talk*, an account of his working life, written by a recently retired engine-driver, Frank McKenna. We shall read more of his experiences later in this chapter. But first we go back nearly a hundred years to Michael Reynolds, a Victorian engineer who published *Engine-driving Life* in 1881, a book based on a lifetime's experience on the rail-

Newly arrived iron ore at Llanwern steel works, South Wales

ways. Here is his account of the terrible fate that befell an engine boy, a working grade that disappeared with compulsory education at the turn of the century:

He left home one bitterly cold winter's night, and his father, mother, and sisters – Nelly and Jinny – remarked before they went to bed what a dreadful night it was. 'We are all at home', said one, 'but our poor little Littleton; he will have a rough time of it.' In the dead of the night, soon after he had taken his supper, an engine-man called him to open the shed-doors, which were closed to keep the cleaners warm, and to keep their torchlamps alight. Littleton had fastened one door back with the catch, and the other he had in the proper position for fastening. The driver, seeing the doors wide open, concluded they were all right, and he put on steam to enter the shed with the engine, tender first. Just as the tender was entering, a gust of wind forced the poor lad and the door, which he could not fasten, against the tender, when he was crushed between the edge of the door and the tender. Although he was mortally wounded, he could speak. He lifted up the arm that was crushed with the other and exclaimed, 'My arm is broken, and my poor father is at home ill in bed!'

Loading mail at night

He was crushed in the shoulder, and taken to the hospital. It was the intention of the surgeons to amputate his arm if he rallied; but he did not rally, and died at the age of fifteen. His sister Zilpah saw him and was frantic with grief, which was intensified by the fact that her brother left home so well. On his funeral card were the appropriate words:

> In perfect health I left my home,
> Not thinking that my time was come.
> In a short time my race was run—
> Weep not, dear friends, God's will be done.

Railway workers in the 1860s

65

Though Michael Reynolds comments that the driver should have sent a fireman to shut the doors, he obviously thought it quite natural to send a boy to do a fireman's work. At that time children were still being exploited, despite Lord Shaftesbury's life work to protect them by law. The basic work of railwaymen changed little in the ninety-odd years after Reynolds's book was published, until the replacement of steam by diesel altered the work for ever. Frank McKenna, whose description of night work opened this chapter, covers much the same ground as Michael Reynolds did nearly a hundred years earlier, but with one difference. Reynolds was an engineer, writing from the outside about firemen and drivers. He told his readers of incidents and adventures which he had not experienced himself. Frank McKenna, however, tells his story from *inside*. He had been through the mill. From him we learn exactly what it was like to fire an engine; the heat endured, the skill and judgement needed, the exhaustion that followed.

Firing a main-line locomotive was generally accepted to be the most laborious of all railway jobs. On a long trip or in high winds, as much as six tons of coal would be shovelled into the locomotive firebox. It was unusual for the fireman to sit down for more than half a minute at a time – many firemen boasted that they never sat down on a four hour run.

The most frightening experience Frank McKenna ever had occurred when he was a fireman, in 1949:

Certainly the worst experience I had was when I was almost burnt to death in a blow-back from a locomotive fire-box in the tunnel at Linslade near Bletchley. I wasn't particularly familiar with the tracks, and I depended on the driver to tell me where I was, where the heavy gradients were, when to stoke harder and when to take it a little bit easy. We breasted the hill at Tring, the driver eased the throttle and we swept down through the Chiltern Hills . . . approaching the tunnel at Linslade. Linslade is a very small tunnel, and only one track runs through it. Going through it on a steam locomotive was always a tense experience. Once the locomotive hit the tunnel the air pressure inside it caused the speed of the train to be checked by as much as thirty miles per hour. As you approached the tunnel the technique was as follows: the dampers were shut on the locomotive, the fire hole doors were closed, the fireman and driver made sure that the front windows of the cab were tightly closed, and held soaking handkerchiefs to their faces. As we entered the tunnel for some reason the driver forgot to open the throttle. The dampers were open, and we were all set for a first-class disaster. It happened. As soon as the locomotive hit the tunnel, as soon as the

66

On the footplate of a steam engine, 1927. Both the fireman and driver can be seen

chimney went under the roof of the tunnel, the down draught and the pressure inside the tunnel forced the fire from the fire-box backwards into the cab. I was standing in the middle of the cab right in front of the fire hole door so I took the full blast of the fire on my face. As it came roaring out of the fire box, I didn't know what had happened; all I knew was that I had to stay there and try to find the valve on the front of the face plate of the locomotive and turn this valve to try and push the fire back in. The result was that I was standing in sheets of flame and my hand was stuck to the brass handle of the nozzle. I stood there with the **flames pouring**, pouring all over me. The tunnel is a short one so the whole thing only took two or three seconds but as we came out of the tunnel I found that the driver had dived into the corner to protect himself and that I had taken the full blast of the blow-back. I had lost my cap, all my hair had been burnt off, all the skin had gone off my face, my clothes were on fire, and all the skin had gone off my hands. This was the way we came out of the tunnel into the night air. The driver brought the train to a standstill at the signal box at Stoke Hammond, and I jumped off. I was terrified, my clothes were still smouldering, and in trying to make my way to the signal box through the darkness I twice tripped over signal wires and fell flat on my face. Eventually I found myself at the top of the stairs of the signal box, and appeared in front of the signal man, burnt and reeking of smoke...He made me sit down and leapt to the telephone. He phoned Bletchley station and said, 'There has been an accident, you had better get an ambulance to Bletchley station.' Then I had to get back into the cab, pick up the shovel again, and put some coal on the fire to get the next two or three miles to Bletchley. When I took my hands away from the shovel I left more skin on the handle.

Frank McKenna was patched up at the hospital, and sent home, arriving in his lodgings at about three o'clock in the morning, where his landlady screamed and ran away when she saw him dressed in white bandages from head to waist. It was a year before the burns cleared up, and the skin on his hands remained for months so soft that if he touched one hand with the other it would bleed. 'So I lived for months with lumps of Elastoplast stuck all over my hands,' he writes. 'I used to go to work like that. After shovelling a bit of coal they would start to bleed again.' It seems incredible that he was not kept in hospital and that he should have had to work when his hands were in such a condition. And this happened less than thirty years ago.

There has always been a romantic aura surrounding engine-drivers, possibly because the danger and responsibility of their job brings them into the same class as soldiers, sailors and airmen. Many of the locomotives they have driven are famous in railway history. These engines have been preserved and can be seen at the Transport Museum in York.

As the engineers and constructors of the nineteenth century laid down the miles of permanent way, and vied with each other to produce the finest and fastest steam locomotives, they inspired the drivers to devote themselves to getting the best out of their engines,

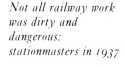

Not all railway work was dirty and dangerous: stationmasters in 1937

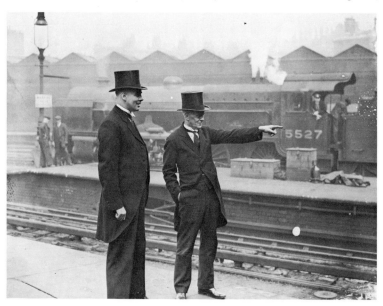

for an engine must be cared for, 'nursed', its temperament studied. The fierce pride which the drivers felt in themselves and their locomotives reached its climax in the stirring races of the last part of the century, races in which timetables were ignored, passengers almost forgotten, and the Company Directors, while pretending that no such thing as a race existed, were no doubt among the crowds that gathered to cheer the drivers on. They set out from the London terminuses of Euston and King's Cross, for the greatest races were those between the North Western and Great Northern Railways, and the most celebrated was the race of 1895.

The west and east routes to Scotland converged at Kinnaber Junction, and after that used the same line on to Aberdeen. Kinnaber Junction lies over the Scottish border, north of Carlisle (the west route) and Newcastle (the east route). Whoever reached Kinnaber first was voted the winner. Aberdeen was still 140 miles away.

The fight started on 22 July 1895. The signalman at Kinnaber was a member of the Caledonian Railway's staff, a Company associated with the North Western, and he was naturally a supporter of the west route. He had the job of letting the victor through Kinnaber Junction by his signals, and he had to be scrupulously fair.

The race was rather biased against the east coast route, for the trains had to travel over the lines of other Companies, whereas the North Western had the advantage of travelling over their own track all the way to Kinnaber. The Great Northern had to make several stops at the bidding of the other Companies whereas the North Western only stopped at Crewe. The staff at Crewe, said Roger Fulford in a B.B.C. broadcast in July 1951, 'did a magnificent job in clearing the vans and pushing on the passengers like greased lightning. One evening a porter, shepherding an old lady into a comfortable seat, was carried off to Carlisle.'

However, the Great Northern at last managed to persuade the North British and North Eastern Companies to forget their time-tables – never mind the passengers – so that a race could be run which would settle the rivalry once and for all, the date chosen being 25 August 1895.

That night the two trains met within one minute of each other, at Kinnaber Junction, and it was not sufficiently a knock-out to satisfy the drivers, so they raced again the following night. This time they arrived at exactly the same moment. When both bells rang simultaneously in the signal box, the signalman had to make a choice

Railwaymen and passengers made good subjects for music-hall songs – and for the covers of the sheet music. So we now have a good record of railway uniforms

– which should be let through first? He after all was a Caledonian, on the side therefore of the North Western. Sportingly he gave his choice to the rival Company. Again the drivers insisted on racing again. The east route won. Yet once again the rivals were spurred on to make a final effort, and this time the west route came in first, a clear victory.

Engine-drivers may have the glory, but guards and porters have their fame too, in numerous ballads and jokes, and above all in the old music-hall songs. A good example of these describes 'The Muddle-Puddle Porter'. On the cover of the music (see page 71) there is a fine drawing, though no artist's name is given. A porter's uniform changed little in a hundred years, and he wore clothes like these until well into the present century. You will notice the bell standing beside his barrow. It was a porter's job to attract attention by ringing a bell and calling the destination of the train just coming in, and the stations at which it was to call, a practice still carried on today, except that there is no bell and the information comes over a loudspeaker, often as difficult to understand as the ludicrous cries of the Muddle-Puddle Porter.

In another, far better-known twentieth-century song, the porter finds himself appealed to by the foolish girl, who sings:

> Oh, Mr Porter, what shall I do?
> I wanted to go to Birmingham,
> And they've carried me on to Crewe!

The Muddle-Puddle Porter

There was a railway porter on the North South Eastern Line,
Whose intellect was limited, whose age was forty-nine.
His post was situated at the Muddle-Puddle Junction.
The stations' names he called out indistinctly – but with unction.
And all this porter had to do thro' morning, noon and night
Was to waggle to and fro a wretched bell with all his might;
And shout this sentence in a manner which you all must know –
'Change here for London, Chatham, Peckham, Brighton, Margate, Bow.'

He thought in all his thirty years of service it was strange
His wages never were increased. 'Twas time to make a change.
He meant to try another calling earlier or later,
So went at once to Spiers and Pond who turned him to a waiter!
But in his new vocation, he in trouble quickly got.
The first old gentlemen who came required a dinner hot,
And asked 'What are the joints?' He said the joints sir, yes, sir, oh!
'The joints are London, Chatham, Peckham, Brighton, Margate, Bow.'

THE MUDDLE-PUDDLE PORTER

He got dismissed and went away in misery and pain,
Determined that he never would a waiter be again;
Such tax upon the intellect would surely make life shorter
He'd still remain the Muddle-Puddle Junction Railway Porter.
And having got his berth again – his spirits did revive
With pride and joy he waited till the first train did arrive.
He rang his bell and shouted out with vigour and with ease –
'Two beefs, a kidney and potatoes, jelly, and a cheese.'

At last the station master said this sort of thing won't do;
'He'd send the Irish mail to smash and call it Irish Stew.
We like originality but do not want a dreamer.'
The porter went as Cabin boy on board a River Steamer.
His duties they were simple for he merely had to shout
Instructions from the Captain, when the boat was turned about.
But when she neared the Temple Pier, he bellowed down below –
'Change here, the joints are Hackney, Kidneys, Peckham, Jelly, Bow.'

The song has two encore verses, in which the porter ends up at the
Hall door of the Westminster Aquarium, calling out:

'Down here for Kidneys, Stepney, Stop her, Jelly, Brighton, Peas,
The tanks are Hackney, turn her stern, Potatoes, Chatham, Cheese.'

The picture of a guard shown here is by an excellent but now
forgotten artist called Alfred Concannon, who supplied many illustrated covers for music-hall songs. On the cover of the song 'The
Railway Guard' Concannon shows a bearded guard wearing the
bandolier of the London and North Western Railway across his
chest. He is standing in front of a green second-class carriage of
that Company – each railway Company had its own livery colours.
In the song, a 'buxom wench, fair, fat and forty' summons the guard
to deal with the gentleman sitting opposite her, who, she swears,
is tickling her legs. The guard soothes her ruffled feelings, and
pulls a basket of live game-fowl from under her seat. It is their
feathers that have been tickling her. The song ends with a warning
and the inevitable pun so dear to Victorian humorists:

ARTHUR LLOYD'S NEW SONG
THE RAILWAY GUARD
OR THE MAIL TRAIN TO THE NORTH

WRITTEN EXPRESSLY FOR HIM BY
GASTON MURRAY   ALFRED PLUMPTON.

> A warning this to young men be, the danger here is shown
> Of riding in a train at night, with a female all alone;
> Look out for baskets 'neath the seat, before you start away,
> Or perhaps you may be accused, one day, of some *foul* play.

In a chapter about engine-drivers, guards and porters we cannot
leave out the touching tale of Snatchburry, an engine-driver's dog,
who won a small place in fame on the London to Rugby run, about

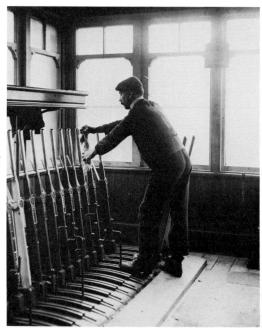

These seven photographs of railwaymen were taken in 1907. Opposite: *engine-driver, signalman, cleaner and ticket-collector.* Above and right: *guard, passenger porter and goods porter*

a hundred years ago. This is recounted by Michael Reynolds in *Engine-driving Life*, published in 1881.

Master Snatchburry was for a period of ten years 'on duty' every day. He sometimes found all his arrangements behind his master's in a morning, and so he had to follow him to the shed, where he would cock up his bright eye first at one engine and then at another, as he ran down the roads between the engines and having found the right one, and some time to spare, he would take a look round and see if anybody was about to offer him a toothful. If he was very late, and he could not just find the engine, his anxiety would increase and intensify his earnestness, until it had worked him into a state of almost convulsive frenzy, making a series of leaps over the pits, to cut off the corners, accompanied by a whining cry developing into a sharp shrill bark. He would sometimes arrive just in time to join the engine when it was leaving the shed for the passenger station; but if he considered the time was too short to join the engine at the shed, he would go direct to the passenger station. On one occasion he came just in time to see his master going away; but, seeing it was a hopeless case, he made no fuss or cry about it, but walked into a quiet spot and dropped down, with the two forefeet straight out before him, indicating health, strength and happiness; and there he lay, taking stock of the trains running in and out of the station, until one came which was going *his* way, the way that would enable him to join his own engine. He would jump onto the engine, work his way to London or Rugby, after Driver Shelvey; and on the engine arriving at the platform, he would take a smart run over the yard from engine to engine until he found the right one.

Snatchburry had learned to distinguish colours; and he distinguished stations from private residences. On seeing a red light he he would bark, and also on approaching a station; but he also knew that a fog-signal indicated extreme danger, and when the wheels of the engine went over some, followed with a *bang, bang*, he would rush frantically round and round the tender, no matter how high the wind was or the speed, or how cold and bleak the air was, in hurricanes of snow and in the midst of perils he called aloud *his* warning high into the air. Driver Shelvey possessed all the knowledge which renders a man fit to run fast and important trains. There were no intricate questions concerning railway working but what he held the thread of; nothing unapproachable, all easy of access, from the leaking of the belly-stay in the boiler to an undeniable breakdown. He ran the most important trains; he ran every trip with success – day after day, for months, for years. His enginemanship was unquestionably sound, and men everywhere knew it – men of authority and experience. Still, on one dark November afternoon, within half an hour after leaving Euston Station with the five o'clock express, his engine was hurled from the iron track right across the other line, over which the engine fell on her side. Shelvey was killed and Snatchburry was saved. As soon as possible search was made for Driver Shelvey among the debris, and he was found with the dog standing by his side; and, following the corpse to the goods-shed, where it was temporarily placed, Snatchburry could only be removed by force.

Buffer: Railway slang

Though the age of the diesel engine has probably destroyed much of it, there has always existed among railwaymen a large number of slang words and expressions. A selection is given here.

Alligator Boots   Boots where the uppers have parted from the sides, due to soaking up diesel oil.

Banjo   A fireman's shovel.

Banker   An engine assisting at the rear of a train going up a steep gradient. 'Bankers' used to mean the navvies, in the days when the railways were being built.

Beetle Crusher   Shunting locomotive in Scottish region.

Beginner's Luck   A driver derailed on his first day in charge of a locomotive.

Bible   Railway Rule Book. Must be carried at all times and be produced on request.

Big Money   Overtime or payment by mileage. This is common on freight trains.

Black Princes   Locomotive-cleaners. In the days of steam, men began as engine-cleaners. The junior member of the gang was given duties underneath the engines. He was gradually promoted to clean the wheels and then the boiler.

Bobbie   A signalman. On early railways the signalman was also a railway policeman, and kept a truncheon in his signal box.

Boomerang   A return ticket.

Bowler Hat Brigade   Railway inspectors. The bowler hat was an emblem of authority until fairly recently.

Coolie   A fireman, who had the hardest job on the railways, and would often be exhausted before he ended the journey, which made it necessary to send another fireman to relieve him.

Crackerjack   A lively foreman.

Dogs   Pincers used for lifting rails and sleepers.

Doggie   Plate-layer, i.e. a man using 'dogs'.

Do-it-yourself Kit   Men working in diesels today use this expression for steam locomotives.

Donkey   A small diesel shunting locomotive.

Down the Nick   Short of steam.

Down the Plug   Water in the engine or the tender running low.

Drum   A tea-can. Drivers and firemen drank tea whenever they could. It could be brewed up in the fire-box at top speed. The fireman would slip the tea-can onto a spanner, balance the

A junction signal in use on the Great Western Railway in 1844

spanner on a shovel and push the whole lot into the fire-box, where the water boiled in a few seconds.

Flea Box   A guard's brake van on a goods train, in the Scottish region. The old vans were very cramped.

Gandy Dancer   A railway plate-layer. Plate-layers keep the rails safe, and work in all weathers. Their work is dangerous and accidents are numerous.

Gnat's Blood   Tea bought from railway canteens or refreshment bars.

Ham   Overtime. 'Fatty ham' is excessive overtime. Railwaymen have never been highly paid and have needed overtime to get themselves a reasonable weekly wage.

Horse and Cart   A slow goods train.

Jungle Juice   Beer.

Liquid Sunshine   Rain.

Needlenoses   Railway auditors whose job is to visit depots and examine the work sheets of guards and drivers, to make sure that their time has been properly used. They are naturally unpopular, but necessary.

Pig-shearing Time   Never.

Shark   Ticket inspector.

Snap   Packed lunch.

Snap Tin   The lunch-box, with a close-fitting lid.

Soap and Towel   A bread-and-cheese meal.

Square Wheels   Anything in a run-down condition, or worn by overwork.

Thin Red Line   A jam sandwich.

Thunder Box   A W.C.

Weezlers   Railway porters, when carrying luggage, are 'weezling', i.e. they do it for a tip.

Yelpers   Railway dogs used for rat-catching. Rats are a great problem in railway yards, tunnels and sidings, for food is often thrown from windows, or swept out of carriages onto the ground. Drivers and firemen have sometimes had to walk through tunnels, and tell terrifying stories of meeting nests of ferocious rats.

Zeppelins   Railway canteen sausages.

Rat-catchers, with their dogs, at St Pancras in 1953. According to British Rail 'the Disinfestation Unit now use more modern methods'

Chapter Five

Tickets please!

The early nineteenth-century railway Companies were formed in the first place to carry goods. It was a surprise to their Directors that passenger traffic increased so rapidly. One reason for this was that the stage coach could carry only eleven passengers at a time; another was the comparative comfort and security of a railway carriage as against the jolting of a coach over muddy, uneven roads, with the danger of a hold-up by highwaymen and footpads on lonely stretches. However, what finally squeezed out the stage-coach services was the speed and cheapness of rail travel – for the passenger himself, for his letters and parcels, his milk and daily newspaper.

We may be too used to jet aeroplanes and inter-city trains to realize what a revolution the first railways brought to society. A lively and informative book, published in 1862, tells us a good deal about rail travel of the time: *The Railway Traveller's Handy Book of Hints, Suggestions and Advice*, author unknown, cost eighteen pence. Early in the book the writer gives some hints on how to catch a train:

If the intention be to start very early in the morning, a vehicle should be engaged. But, by the time the vehicle arrives, you yourselves should be ready to step into it. To this end, it will be necessary to ask a policeman to call you at the proper hour. In some country towns the people who have to attend the markets are in the habit of chalking opposite to their doors overnight, the hour at which they wish to be aroused the next morning. Thus the policeman reads his instructions as he walks his beat, and awakens the inmates accordingly. This hint might be acted upon by railway travellers.

Railway food has always been the butt of jokes and criticism. The great Brunel complained bitterly of the catering at Swindon, an

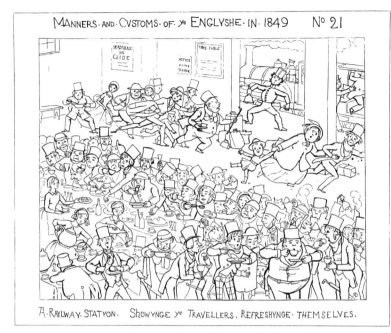

MANNERS·AND·CVSTOMS·OF·Yᵉ ENGLYSHE·IN·1849   Nº 21

A·RAYLWAY·STATYON· SHOWYNGE Yᵉ TRAVELLERS·REFRESHYNGE·THEMSELVES·

Railway food in 1849, as seen by cartoonist Richard Doyle

important station on his own Great Western Railway. He once wrote to the man in charge of providing food and drink there:

Dear Sir,

I assure you Mr Player was wrong in supposing that I thought you purchased inferior coffee. I thought I said to him that I was surprised you should buy such bad roasted corn. I did not believe you had such a thing as coffee in the place; I am certain that I never tasted any. I have long ceased to make complaints at Swindon. I avoid taking anything there when I can help it.

Yours faithfully,
I. K. Brunel.

But a glowing account of the London and Birmingham Railway Station at Wolverton is given by Sir Francis Bond Head in *Stokers and Pokers*, published in 1850. He lists the large number of staff employed in the Wolverton refreshment establishment: a matron; seven very young ladies to wait on passengers; four men and three boys ditto; one man-cook, his kitchen-maid, and two scullery-maids; two housemaids; one still-room maid, employed solely in the 'liquid duty of making tea and coffee'; two laundry-maids and one baker's boy; one garden boy, and lastly, an 'odd-man'.

There were evidently some serious hazards in early rail travel as

The silver coffee-pot in the shape of an engine which produced the 'coffee' that inspired Brunel's letter

the following alarming story, from a book called *Railway Economy*, published in 1850, relates. The author, the Countess of Zetland, was travelling in her own carriage.

On the 8th of Dec I left Darlington by the 9h 25m train for London. I travelled in my chariot with my maid. The carriage was strapped onto a truck and placed with its back to the engine, about the centre of the train, which was a long one. Soon after leaving Leicester I thought I smelt something burning and told my maid to look out of the window on her side to see if anything was on fire. She let down the window, and so many lumps of red-hot coal or coke were showering down that she put it up again immediately. I still thought I smelt something burning; she put down the window again and exclaimed that the carriage was on fire. We then put down the side-windows and waved our handkerchiefs, scream-ing 'fire' as loud as we could. No one took any notice of us. I then pulled up the windows, lest no current of air through the carriage should cause the fire to burn more rapidly into the carriage, and determined to sit in as long as possible. After some time, seeing that no assistance was likely to be afforded us, my maid became terrified, and without telling me her intention, opened the door, let down the step, and scrambled out onto the truck. I followed her, but having unluckily let myself down towards the back part of the carriage, which was on fire, was obliged to put up the step and close the door as well as I could to enable me to pass to the front part of the carriage, furthest from the fire, and where my maid was standing. We clung on by the front springs of the carriage, screaming 'fire' incessantly, and waving our handkerchiefs. We passed several policemen on the road, none of whom took any notice of us. No guard appeared. A gentleman in the carriage behind mine saw us, but could render no assistance. My maid seemed in an agony of terror, and I saw her sit down on the side of the truck and gather her cloak tightly about her. I think I told her to hold fast to the carriage. I turned away for a moment to wave my handkerchief, and when I looked round again my poor maid was gone. The train went on, the fire of course increasing, and the wind blowing it towards me. A man (a passenger) crept along the ledge of the railway carriages and came as near as possible to the truck on which I stood, but it was impossible for him to help me. At last the train stopped at the Rugby Station. An engine was sent back to find my maid. She was found on the road and taken to Leicester hospital, where she now lies in an almost hopeless state; her skull fractured; three of her fingers have been amputated. I am told the train was going at the rate of 50 miles an hour.

A less frightening but very bizarre adventure befell another young lady travelling alone. The story is told in *Railway Adventures and Anecdotes*, published in 1884.

After I had taken my seat one morning at Paddington, in an empty carriage, I was joined, just as the train was moving off, by a strange-looking young man, with remarkably long flowing hair. He was, of course, a little hurried, but he seemed besides to be so disturbed and wild that I was quite alarmed, for fear of his not being in his right mind, nor did his subsequent conduct at all reassure me. Our train was an express, and he inquired, eagerly, at once, which was the first station we were advertised to stop. I consulted my Bradshaw and furnished him with the required information. It was Reading. The young man looked at his watch. 'Madam,' said he, 'I have but half an hour between me, and, it may be, ruin. Excuse, therefore, my abruptness. You have, I perceive, a pair of scissors in your workbag. Oblige me, if you please, by cutting off all my hair.'

'Sir,' said I, 'it is impossible.'

'Madam,' he urged, and a look of severe determination crossed his features; 'I am a desperate man. Beware how you refuse me what I ask. Cut my hair off–short, close to the roots–immediately; and here is a newspaper to hold the ambrosial curls.'

I thought he was mad, of course; and believing that it would be dangerous to thwart him, I cut off all his hair to the last lock.

'Now, madam,' said he, unlocking a small portmanteau, 'you will further oblige me by looking out of the window, as I am about to change my clothes.'

Of course I looked out of the window for a very considerable time,

81

Top left: *a coach on an early Stockton–Darlington train. Second-class coaches were not upholstered till 1854 – the same year in which third-class coaches were roofed*

Top right: *seated in the luxury of a first-class carriage, 1867*

Below left: *a saloon carriage on the London–Brighton line, 1873*

Below right: *'Off for the holiday', 1877*

Left: *a dining car on the Great Northern Railway, 1879*

Below: *a Pullman sleeper on the Midland Railway, 1874. Sleeping cars came to Britain in 1873, but Pullman sleepers, which were more luxurious, did not arrive till the following year*

and when he observed, 'Madam, I need no longer put you to any inconvenience,' I did not recognize the young man in the least.

Instead of his former rather gay costume, he was attired in black, and wore a grey wig and silver spectacles; he looked like a respectable divine of the Church of England, of about sixty-four years of age; to complete that character, he held a volume of sermons in his hand, which – they appeared so to absorb him – might have been his own.

'I do not wish to threaten you, young lady,' he resumed, 'and I think, besides, that I can trust your kind face. Will you promise me not to reveal this metamorphosis until your journey's end?'

'I will,' said I, 'most certainly.'

At Reading, the guard and a person in plain clothes looked into our carriage.

'You have the ticket, my love,' said the young man, blandly, and looking to me as though he were my father.

'Never mind, sir; we don't want them,' said the official, as he withdrew with his companion.

'I shall now leave you, madam,' observed my fellow-traveller, as soon as the coast was clear; 'by your kind and courageous conduct you have saved my life and, perhaps, even your own.'

In another minute he was gone, and the train was in motion. Not till the next morning did I learn from *The Times* newspaper that the gentleman on whom I had operated as hair cutter had committed a forgery to an enormous amount, in London, a few hours before I met him, and that he had been tracked into the express train from Paddington; but that – although the telegraph had been put in motion and described him accurately – at Reading, when the train was searched, he was nowhere to be found.

Britain was slow to improve railway carriages for the better comfort of travellers, but it is hardly surprising that the matter was more seriously regarded in America, with the huge distances that many had to travel. The U.S.A. carried out an immense railway-building programme between about 1835 and 1890. After teething troubles the system became super-efficient. For the first time thousands of ordinary American citizens began to know their vast country a little better, though some complained that the railway guides didn't always give a true picture. A citizen from the eastern States, persuaded to explore the far west by railroad, made a bitter complaint to G. A. Sala, which the latter records in his book, *America Revisited*:

There ain't no bottling up of things about me. This overland journey's a fraud, and you oughter know it. Don't tell me. It's a fraud. This Ring

An early poster advertising the Union Pacific

must be busted up. Where are your buffalers? Perhaps you'll tell me that them cows is buffalers. They ain't. Where are your prairie dogs? They ain't dogs to begin with, they're squirrels. Ain't you ashamed to call the mean little cusses dogs? But where are they? There ain't none? Where are your grizzlies? You might have imported a few grizzlies to keep up the name of your railroad. Where are your herds of antelopes scudding before the advancing train? Nary an antelope have you got for to send. Rocky Mountains, sir? They ain't rocky at all – they're as flat as my hand. Where are your savage gorges? I can't see none. Where are your wild injuns? Do you call them loafing tramps in dirty blankets, injuns? My belief is that they are greasers looking out for an engagement as song and dance men. They're 'beats', sir, 'dead beats', they're 'pudcocks', and you oughter be told so.

The kitchen of an American Pullman car – an illustration from Sala's book

The American designers built quite different carriages from those in Britain. Their 'passenger cars' were long, with central gangways, and heating stoves. As early as 1859 Pullman's first sleeping-car conversions were on the rails, and, ten years later, Westinghouse's compressed-air brakes were in use, an important step forward in safety soon adopted by other countries. Pullman's sixteen-wheeled 'Pioneer' became the model car for American trains, especially after the original model had been chartered for President Lincoln's funeral train. Pullman also developed the restaurant car and by the 1870s his cars were rolling across the States to San Francisco on the Pacific coast. Rich men owned Pullman cars as they own aeroplanes today. They were 'mansions on wheels', over ninety feet long, and contained almost every luxury except a swimming-pool: 'open grates, harmoniums, portable mushroom farms, printing presses and Jersey cattle to provide fresh milk ... and legions of servants'. In 1930 there were nearly 10,000 Pullman cars in the U.S.A., consuming four million cakes of soap a year, with a laundry bill of over three million dollars!

Another view from Sala's book of an American Pullman

It sounds luxurious, but Charles Dickens gained a very different impression of American railroads when he visited the U.S.A. in 1842. The following extract is taken from his book *American Notes*:

There are no first- and second-class carriages as with us; but there is a gentlemen's car and a ladies' car: the main distinction between which is that in the first, everybody smokes; and in the second, nobody does. As a black man never travels with a white one, there is also a negro car; which is a great, blundering, clumsy chest, such as Gulliver put to sea in, from the kingdom of Brobdingnag. There is a great deal of jolting, a great deal of noise, a great deal of wall, not much window, a locomotive engine, a shriek, and a bell.

85

*A Pullman smoking car,
around 1900*

The cars are like shabby omnibuses, but larger: holding thirty, forty,
fifty people. The seats, instead of stretching from end to end, are placed
crosswise. Each seat holds two persons. There is a long row of them on
each side of the caravan, a narrow passage up the middle, and a door at
both ends. In the centre of the carriage there is usually a stove, fed
with charcoal or anthracite coal; which is for the most part red-hot. It
is insufferably close; and you see the hot air fluttering between your-
self and any other object you may happen to look at, like the ghost of
smoke.

In the ladies' car, there are a great many gentlemen who have ladies
with them. There are also a great many ladies who have nobody with
them: for any lady may travel alone, from one end of the United
States to the other, and be certain of the most courteous and considerate
treatment everywhere. The conductor or checktaker, or guard, or whatever he may be, wears no uniform. He walks up and down the car, and
in and out of it, as his fancy dictates; leans against the door with his
hands in his pockets and stares at you, if you chance to be a stranger;
or enters into conversation with the passengers about him. A great many
newspapers are pulled out, and a few of them are read. Everybody talks
to you, or to anybody else who hits his fancy. If you are an Englishman,
he expects that that railroad is pretty much like an English railroad.
If you say 'No', he says 'Yes?' (interrogatively), and asks in what
respect they differ. You enumerate the heads of difference, one by one,
and he says 'Yes?' (still interrogatively) to each. Then he guesses that

*Passengers settling for
the night on an
American train*

you don't travel faster in England; and on your replying that you do,
says 'Yes?' again (still interrogatively), and, it is quite evident, don't
believe it. After a long pause he remarks, partly to you, and partly to
the knob on the top of his stick, that 'Yankees are reckoned to be considerable of a go-ahead people too'; upon which *you* say 'Yes', and then
he says 'Yes' again (affirmatively this time); and upon your looking out
of the window, tells you that behind that hill, and some three miles from
the next station, there is a clever town in a smart lo-ca-tion, where he
expects you have con-cluded to stop. Your answer in the negative
naturally leads to more questions in reference to your intended route
(always pronounced rout); and wherever you are going, you invariably
learn that you can't get there without immense difficulty and danger,
and that all the great sights are somewhere else.

If a lady take a fancy to any male passenger's seat, the gentleman who
accompanies her gives him notice of the fact, and he immediately vacates
it with great politeness. Politics are much discussed, so are banks, so is
cotton. Quiet people avoid the question of the President, for there will
be a new election in three years and a half, and party feeling runs very
high: the great constitutional feature of this institution being, that
directly the acrimony of the last election is over, the acrimony of the
next one begins; which is an unspeakable comfort to all strong politicians
and true lovers of their country: that is to say, to ninety-nine men and
boys out of every ninety-nine and a quarter.

Except when a branch road joins the main one, there is seldom more
than one track of rails; so that the road is very narrow, and the view,

where there is a deep cutting, by no means extensive. When there is not, the character of the scenery is always the same. Mile after mile of stunted trees: some hewn down by the axe, some blown down by the wind, some half fallen and resting on their neighbours, many mere logs half hidden in the swamp, others mouldered away to spongy chips. The very soil of the earth is made up of minute fragments such as these; each pool of stagnant water has its crust of vegetable rottenness; on every side there are the boughs, and trunks, and stumps of trees, in every possible stage of decay, decomposition, and neglect. Now you emerge for a few brief minutes on an open country, glittering with some bright lake or pool, broad as many an English river, but so small here that it scarcely has a name; now catch hasty glimpses of a distant town, with its clean white houses and their cool piazzas, its prim New England church and schoolhouse; when whir-r-r-r! almost before you have seen them, comes the same dark screen: the stunted trees, the stumps, the logs, the stagnant water – all so like the last that you seem to have been transported back again by magic.

The train calls at stations in the woods, where the wild impossibility of anybody having the smallest reason to get out, is only to be equalled by the apparently desperate hopelessness of there being anybody to get in. It rushes across the turnpike road, where there is no gate, no policeman, no signal: nothing but a rough wooden arch, on which is painted 'WHEN THE BELL RINGS, LOOK OUT FOR THE LOCOMOTIVE'. On it whirls headlong, dives through the woods again, emerges in the light, clatters over frail arches, rumbles upon the heavy ground, shoots beneath a wooden bridge which intercepts the light for a second like a wink, suddenly awakens all the slumbering echoes in the main street of a large town, and dashes on haphazard, pell-mell, neck-or-nothing, down the middle of the road. There – with mechanics working at their trades, and people leaning from their doors and windows, and boys flying kites and playing marbles, and men smoking, and women talking, and children crawling, and pigs burrowing, and unaccustomed horses plunging and rearing, close to the very rails – there – on, on, on – tears the mad dragon of an engine with its train of cars; scattering in all directions a shower of burning sparks from its wood fire; screeching, hissing, yelling, panting; until at last the thirsty monster stops beneath a covered way to drink, the people cluster round, and you have time to breathe again.

If Dickens found America's comparatively modern trains so uncomfortable, it is as well that he never travelled in Australia, where passenger comfort was one of the last things to be considered. Australia was late in building railways. *The Australian Book of Trains* begins with the statement: 'The two main essentials required

for the building of a railroad are a lot of money and a wheel-barrow.' Although Australia was a poor country in the mid-nine-teenth century, she had plenty of men, many of them ex-convicts, to hump the barrows, and in July 1850 New South Wales laid down the first section of track, linking Sydney with the settlements inland. The last of the Australian states to build a railroad was the sparsely populated Northern Territory. Ernestine Hill, in her book *The Great Australian Loneliness*, describes travelling on this early and somewhat primitive railroad.

I left for Darwin on the 'Sentinel', 'First Ladies'. There is a train a week in the Territory, and it runs practically the whole gamut of Terri-tory history and scenery. All the natives of the countryside put on their dungarees and Mother Hubbards, and straggle down to the sidings to watch it go through and old settlers, camped on the creeks, rectify their calendars by its whistle. They call it 'Leaping Lena'. One terminus is Birdum, three shacks in the bush, and the other the first breakers of the Indian Ocean ...

In the pungent wet season it was here that I began to smell the Terri-tory, Chinese scents of lancewood, and steaming lagoons and jungle grasses, blacks and pandanus, and later the reek of the mangrove creeks and crocodile rivers. The 'Sentinel' – 'Leaping Lena's' official name – is a string of scarcely glorified cattle trucks that never fails to provide a good jest at the expense of overland travellers. So uncomfortable are

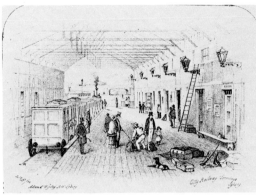

The Great Zigzag near Lithgow, New South Wales, was an engineering masterpiece. It provided a descent from the Blue Mountains on a grade of 1 in 42 by three graceful sweeps on the side of a deep ravine

The Sydney terminus, by Samuel Thomas Gill in his Scenery In and Around Sydney, *1856*

Two stretches of line on the Melbourne and Hobson's Bay Railway

its narrow wooden seats that those who know them always prefer to sit on the floor. But there is a humour and a hearty democracy about it that no other train in Australia can boast. The guard has been known to bring round 'beer for all aboard' on the Sentinel.

Passengers are as varied a collection of human oddities as the world can offer – buffalo-hunters and anthropologists, mining agents and half-castes, A.I.M. sisters on errands of mercy bent, white men seeking medical attention for spear-wounds, globe-trotters and stockmen, Russian peanut-farmers and Chinese women in their national dress, with frequently a tribe making down to Darwin for 'big-fella corroboree' in the compound there.

We pulled in for the night at Pirie Creek, where the grasshoppers are as big as birds and the frogs have voices like goats ... On went the little train, through the towering grasses and swamps of the wet season, past the Adelaide and Darwin rivers, and then twenty miles through a thick jungle of eucalyptus and milk-wood and fan-palm and sago-palm and screw-palm, to pull in beside a pearling-camp on the Indian Ocean, and wake Darwin from siesta with its shrill little whistle, in time for afternoon tea.

First Class

2s. 6d. LUNCHEON

MENU.

February 14th, 1898.

Printanier.

Grilled Turbot.

Roast Sirloin Beef.
Vegetables.

Bread and Butter Pudding.

Cheese.

TO ORDER A LA CARTE.

FISH.

Salmon Sauce Hollandaise.

COLD.	FROM THE GRILL.
Roast Beef.	Mutton Chop.
Chicken and Ham.	Mutton Cutlets (2).
Roast Lamb.	Rump Steak.
Roast Mutton.	Chicken and Bacon.

FRUIT EXTRA.

Apple Tart.   Crème Caramel.

Coffee per Cup, with Luncheon or Dinner
extra 4d.

DINING CAR SERVICE
LUNCHEON (1 Dollar)
Consommé with Rice
Chicken Bouillon in Cups
Olives   Celery
Fried Smelts, Tartar Sauce
Potato Chips
Curry of Chicken, with Rice
Veal Cutlet, Breaded, Tomato Sauce
Omelette, with Asparagus
Roast Beef
Browned Potatoes
Shrimp Salad   Chicken Salad
Cold Roast Beef   Tongue   Sardines
Boston Baked Beans
Potatoes in Cream   Mashed Potatoes
Baked Sweet Potatoes
String Beans   New Beets
Baked Stuffed Tomatoes
Lettuce, with Egg. French dressing
Rice Custard Pudding
Ice Cream   Pies   Assorted Cakes
Dundee Marmalade   Gingerbread
Fruit in Season
Edam, Roquefort, Canadian Paragon Cheese
Graham Wafers   Bent's Water Crackers
Preserved Fruit
Cocoa   Coffee

Railway menus from Britain and the United States at the turn of the century

Chapter Six

Railway accidents

There is more to a railway disaster than thrills and drama. Accidents are the responsibility of *someone*, and it is extraordinary to read of the indifference to safety devices shown by nineteenth-century railway Companies. George Stephenson, very early on, found his advice on safety ignored, and it needed several really serious accidents to shock the railway Directors into spending money to ensure safe travelling.

Two of the most valuable safety devices developed during the nineteenth century were the fitting of continuous brakes (i.e. brakes connected from carriage to carriage, which could be applied instantly by driver or guard and acted on every wheel) and the 'block' system. This was a means of dividing every railway line into 'train-tight' compartments, so that only *one* train at a time could be running on any one stretch of the track. The companies were so lax about imposing this discipline, however, that it took over fifty years and many serious accidents before the lesson was fully learned. It was only in 1889 that block-working and continuous brakes were made compulsory by the Government.

The first major accident on British railways occurred on Christmas Eve, 1841, in Sonning railway cutting in Berkshire. Heavy rain had brought down a mass of earth onto the railway track. At this time third-class carriages were little better than cattle trucks. They had no sides and no buffers. Seats were merely planks. The 'lower orders' travelled immediately behind the engine and tender, justifiably considered the least safe place on the train. On Christmas Eve 1841 two third-class carriages full of workmen returning home for Christmas had been coupled immediately behind the engine and tender. Behind them came a parcels van and then seventeen heavy-goods wagons.

When the engine ran full tilt into the 'slip', the pile of earth fallen onto the line in the cutting, not only did the first two carriages run straight into the tender in front, but the goods wagons piled up and crushed them from behind. The number of dead was eight. In 1841 communications were so primitive that it was some time before medical aid could be brought for the injured. Ironically the openness of the carriages was a mercy in this case, as many men were thrown clear.

Two important results of this early accident were that improvements were begun on third-class carriages, and that the practice of mixing passenger and goods wagons on the same train was condemned, though not entirely abandoned for many years.

Tunnels, which had always been a source of dread to nervous passengers, were given safeguards fairly early, yet Britain's worst rail disaster in the first fifty years of railway history occurred in a tunnel, the Claydon tunnel on the London, Brighton and South Coast Railway.

This tunnel had a 'block' system worked by electric telegraph, and operated by signalmen at each end. This was designed expressly to prevent more than one train at a time ever going through the tunnel. Yet the system failed. This was not really due to the telegraph 'block' system in itself. The intervals between three trains were not sufficiently long, nor did the drivers keep strictly to their timetable. A minimum of five minutes between trains leaving a station was the rule, but this was too short, and made no allowance for human error or variations in timing due to weather conditions, etc. On 25 August 1861 three heavily laden trains left Brighton within a few minutes of each other. Two of them were excursion trains full of holiday-makers. They plodded through Sussex towards the downs and the tunnel, with only *three to four minutes* between them.

Signalman Killich was on duty at the south end of the Claydon tunnel. He had a simple electric telegraph with which to communicate with his opposite number, Signalman Brown at Claydon Tunnel North.

The first train, an excursion bound for Portsmouth, entered the tunnel, but the signal failed to work. It remained stuck at ALL CLEAR. The bell should have sounded but, if it did, Killich never heard it. He sent his usual 'train in tunnel' telegraph signal to Brown, then turned round to see to his horror another train about to enter the tunnel close behind the first – packed with passengers,

for it too was an excursion. He snatched up his red flag and un-
furled it just as engine number two disappeared into the tunnel.
He then rushed to his telegraph and sent to Brown a second 'train
in tunnel' warning, adding: 'Is tunnel now clear?' Brown received
this message and question just as train number one burst out of the
tunnel in a cloud of smoke, and passed his cabin. He signalled
back to Killich 'ALL CLEAR'. But of course it was not all clear, for
train number two was still in the tunnel. Did Brown never receive
the second message? The system easily led to confusion in special
circumstances like this. Meanwhile Killich thought that all was now
well, took in his red flag and put out a white one to indicate the
tunnel was clear.

The third train now appeared, an ordinary regular passenger train.
It speeded into the tunnel and its driver waved cheerfully to Killich
as he went in. But what had happened to number two train, which
we last heard of entering the tunnel? Its driver, Scott, had just
caught the flicker of a red flag as he took his train into the tunnel.
Driving on in the pitch darkness, he was worried. He decided to
shut off steam, and his fireman screwed down the brake. The train
was heavy and was carried half a mile into the tunnel before it came
to a standstill. Scott felt suspicious that there might be something
wrong ahead of him and began cautiously backing his train. About
250 yards from the tunnel entrance train number three, the regular
Brighton train, crashed straight into it. The engine ploughed
through the rear coach of number two excursion train and, after
smashing the guard's van to pieces (the guard jumped clear), it
reared up like a horse, till the chimney hit the roof and broke
off. Onto the wreckage beneath it there poured a mass of red-hot
coals, and steam escaping from broken pipes enveloped the wreckage. Of the twenty-three passengers who died, most of them were
in this rear coach. One hundred and seventy-six people were injured
seriously.

This terrible accident brought a storm of criticism against the
railway Company concerned, against its inefficient instruments for
signalling, and its overworked signalmen. But the London, Brighton
and South Coast Railway Board of Directors was unmoved. Superintendent John Chester Craven wrote: 'My board feel bound to
state frankly that they have not seen reason to alter the views
which they have so long entertained on this subject.' Not only was
the toll of life heavy and the number of injured considerable, most
of the victims had suffered horribly, and the public was shocked.

Nothing shook the bland assurance of the Directors and their Superintendent, however. Mr Craven crowned his defence of the Company by stating that in his opinion the more safety devices you use, the less safety you have!

The 1860s brought to railway records an accident notable for the distinguished writer involved in it. On 9 June 1865 the boat train from Folkestone met with a stretch of line under repair, which had been left most improperly signalled. Matters had been made worse by the fact that the foreman of the plate-layers consulted the wrong page in his timetable, and thought the Folkestone train was due at 5.20 p.m., when it was in fact due at 3.11 p.m. The work was being done on the approach to a bridge over the river Beult. Two rails had been taken up, and the engine ran over the gap in the track, pulling the whole train after it, and eight of its fourteen carriages were derailed and fell over the bridge into the river. One carriage hung over the bridge, but fortunately did not fall. In it was Charles Dickens, returning from France. Here is his account of what happened, written to a friend, Thomas Mitton:

Tuesday, June 13th, 1865

My dear Mitton,

I should have written to you yesterday or the day before, if I had been quite up to writing.

I was in the only carriage that did not go over into the stream. It was caught upon the turn by some of the ruin of the bridge, and hung

This sketch was taken at Staplehurst, the scene of the accident, on the following day

suspended and balanced in an apparently impossible manner. Two ladies were my fellow-passengers, an old one and young one. This is exactly what passed. Suddenly we were off the rail, and beating the ground as the car of a half-emptied balloon might. The old lady cried out, 'My God!' and the young one screamed. I caught hold of them both and said: 'We can't help ourselves, but we can be quiet and composed. Pray don't cry out.' The old lady immediately answered: 'Thank you. Rely on me. Upon my soul I will be quiet.' We were then all tilted down together in a corner of the carriage. I said to them: 'Will you remain here without stirring, while I get out of the window?' They both answered quite collectedly, 'Yes' and I got out without the least notion what had happened. Fortunately I got out with great caution and stood upon the step. Looking down I saw the bridge gone, and nothing below me but the line of rail. The two guards (one with his face cut) were running up and down on the down side of the bridge (which was not torn up) quite wildly. I called out to them: 'Look at me. Do stop an instant and look at me, and tell me whether you don't know me.' One of them answered: 'We know you very well, Mr Dickens.' 'Then,' I said, 'my good fellow, for God's sake give me your key and I'll empty this carriage.' We did it quite safely, by means of a plank or two, and when it was done I saw all the rest of the train, except the two baggage-vans down in the stream. I got into the carriage again for my brandy flask, took off my travelling hat for a basin, climbed down the brickwork, and filled my hat with water.

Suddenly I came upon a staggering man covered with blood, with such a frightful cut across the skull that I couldn't bear to look at him. I poured some water over his face and gave him some to drink, then gave him some brandy, and laid him down on the grass, and he said, 'I am gone,' and died afterwards. Then I stumbled over a lady lying on her back against a little pollard-tree, with the blood streaming over her face (which was lead colour). I asked her if she could swallow a little brandy and she just nodded, and I gave her some and left her for somebody else. The next time I passed her she was dead. No imagination can conceive the ruin of the carriages, or the extraordinary weights under which the people were lying, or the complications into which they were twisted up among iron and wood, and mud and water.

I don't want to be examined at the inquest, and I don't want to write about it. I could do no good either way, and I could only seem to speak about myself, which, of course, I would rather not do.

Ever faithfully,
Charles Dickens.

The accident made a profound impression upon Dickens, and affected his already deteriorating health. He was so nervous in trains that he positively writhed in agony if travelling at any speed. He

Dickens finds the injured lady

was giving lecture tours and readings at the time, and suffering from lack of sleep and fainting fits. Late in 1867 he went to the States to lecture, and could only keep going on a highly alcoholic diet: cream and rum for breakfast, sherry-cobbler during the morning, a pint of champagne at 3 p.m., an egg in sherry before his reading, and afterwards soup, wine and often laudanum, a powerful sleeping drug. He returned to England, and died in 1870, five years after the Staplehurst accident, and on the very date of it: 9 June.

Carelessness, indeed gross negligence, was the cause of the worst disaster in British rail history, the Quintinhill blaze of 1915, 'when a signalman forgot; three trains collided and more than two hundred people died'. The Great War of 1914 to 1918 was at the end of its first year. Quintinhill lies near the Scottish border north of Carlisle, a lonely spot with no station or village, just two loops in the single railway line to allow for passing, and a signal box from which a solitary signalman controls the traffic. No doubt it was easy for a man on duty there to feel bored, possibly tired or sleepy. The signalmen at that time had certainly become slack, and they stretched the rules to suit themselves, not always keeping to strict times, for instance. It might have worked perfectly well for years, but on this particular morning the unexpected happened and the signalmen were not ready for it. A train packed with troops was coming up from Carlisle early in the morning, and at Quintinhill it rammed into a local with such force that many of the carriages were smashed to matchwood. Only a few minutes later, while all was confusion in the signal box and on the line, an express from Carlisle ran straight into the wreckage and into the soldiers who were trying to get out of their smashed carriages. Here is an eye-witness account from an unnamed man living in a near-by cottage, reported in J. A. B. Hamilton's *Britain's Greatest Rail Disaster*:

I was just finishing breakfast when I was startled by a terrific crash. I did not know what had caused it, but surmising that something terrible had happened on the railway I rushed from the house, and looking towards the line I was horrified to see the express dash into a mass of wreckage. I realized then what had been the cause of the crash that I had heard at breakfast. A collision had already taken place, and I was just in time to witness the second.

I had scarcely grasped the horror of it all when I was appalled to observe the whole mass of wreckage burst into flames. A dreadful quietness seemed to hang over the place for a second or two, and then I saw

'I was horrified to see the express dash into a mass of wreckage'

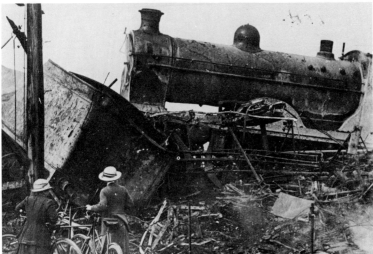

'In a moment all was terrible confusion'

figures running and crawling from the wreck. I dashed across the field to render what assistance I could, but before I reached the embankment the flames had got hold of the smashed carriages.

And here are the words of a reporter who questioned the soldiers in the troop train:

When the first shock was received the sergeant in charge of the compartment gave the order to hold tight, and the men stood on the seats

99

and clung desperately to the luggage racks as the carriages appeared to be toppling over. The awful force of the second collision then burst upon them. In a moment all was terrible confusion. Engines were heaped upon one another, carriages telescoped and overturned, and others mounted one upon the other. Men were hurled from the train – a fortunate few well clear – others clambered out from the wreckage as best they could. Many were pinned below the overturned carriages. Already the troop train and the leading carriages of the London train were ablaze. The men still on board were in a terrible plight. The successive collisions had effectively jammed the carriage doors. Exit that way was impossible. Windows refused to come down, and the glass had to be smashed before the men could get clear. Many men confessed that they did not know by what means or in what manner they got out. 'The great thing is, we got out,' said one man, 'and we thank God we got clear of yon hell.'

It then took more than an hour for an emergency train to bring ambulance staff and doctors to Quintinhill. The fire brigade was not even informed to start with. When at last it was summoned, the men had to run their hoses half a mile away to the river Sark, for water.

How many people died in the accident? The exact number is not known, but the figure usually given is 227.

Fortunately, not all accidents have such dreadful consequences. On 4 August 1936 a Somerset and Dorset Joint Railway tank engine was shunting at a colliery sidings at Radstock in Somerset.

One of the trucks that shot over the embankment at Midford

The engine-driver looked out of his cab to see a freight train – and a very heavy one – approaching along the line he was on. It had overrun the signals and, what was worse, its engine-crew had leaped off the footplate. Fortunately it was moving slowly. The driver of the tank engine flung his engine into back gear, and 'ran away' from the freight train as best he could, but it gained slowly upon him until eventually its engine met his, nose to nose, but without actually colliding. The driver had the presence of mind to leap out of his own cab, jump into the other and bring it to a complete halt. Unfortunately, however, his own fireman was a nervous fellow, who had jumped out of the tank engine cab on the other side from the driver and the engine was now slowly moving backwards, with no one at the controls. Neither man had closed the regulator to bring the engine to a stop, and the driver saw his own engine disappearing in the direction of Bath, pushing eight wagons in front of it. And it was gathering speed as it went. It roared through Wellow station at fifty m.p.h., ran amok on the points at Midford where, to quote L. T. C. Rolt, 'Signals and telegraph poles fell like ninepins; signalman Larcombe's cabin collapsed under his feet as one wagon demolished its masonry base; six wagons shot one after another over an embankment ... yet No. 7620 [the tank engine] held to the rails and her powers were by no means exhausted. Having so successfully shaken off most of her load she continued at unabated speed, pushing before her like a handcart the remnant of one wagon running on two wheels only. Miraculously she succeeded in propelling this peculiar vehicle through Combe Down and Devonshire single line tunnels, but at Claude Avenue overbridge it brought about her undoing. The remaining end door of the wagon fell off, got under her rear wheels and derailed her. At about the same time the fusible plug in the crown of her firebox melted owing to shortage of water and her last breath was spent. The escapade was over.'

The demolished signal box

Buffer: An engine-driver's epitaph

My engine is now cold and still,
No water does my boiler fill,
My coke affords its flame no more,
My days of usefulness are o'er,
My wheels deny their noted speed,
No more my guiding hand they heed;
My whistle – it has lost its tone,
Its shrill and thrilling sound is gone;
My valves are now thrown open wide,
My flanges all refuse to glide;
My clacks – alas! though once so strong,
Refuse their aid in the busy throng;
No more I feel each urging breath,
My steam is now condensed in death;
Life's railway o'er, each station past,
In death I'm stopped, and rest at last.

This epitaph is inscribed on a tombstone at Alton, Illinois. The man was an engineer on the old Chicago and Mississippi Railroad. He was fatally injured in an accident and is said to have written these lines while awaiting death.

Chapter Seven

Heroes and heroines

Almost every country has its railway heroes and heroines. The dangers of war have made special demands upon the courage and resourcefulness of railwaymen, and it is the story of a wartime hero that begins this chapter.

The time is just after midnight on 2 June 1944, towards the end of the Second World War. The place is near the east coast of England, where an engine-driver called Benjamin Gimbert is detailed to take a trainload of bombs across the dark flat country of the Fens. He has forty 500-lb bombs in the first wagon, seventy-four more in the second, a load of detonators in the third, and after that forty-eight more wagons all filled with high explosives.

Driver Gimbert and his fireman start off just after midnight and all goes well until they approach the small town of Soham, near Cambridge, with its splendid old church and four windmills. Gimbert leans out of his cab and sees to his horror that the first wagon is on fire. He and his mate can save their own lives by jumping clear, but Gimbert knows that his train is carrying enough explosives to blast the town to rubble. He pulls up before he reaches Soham station. His mate leaps down and runs back, to uncouple the burning wagon from the fifty behind it. Then Gimbert drives on through and past the station, hoping to get clear of the town before uncoupling his engine from wagon Number One. He hails the signalman, to ask if the line is clear ahead, but there's no answer, for at that moment the wagon blows up.

The cool courage of Driver Gimbert saved the town and earned him the George Cross, but the force of the explosion flung him over the rails to the far platform, and he was seriously injured. The signalman and fireman were both killed, the latter being

Benjamin Gimbert

Spirit of Protest

awarded the George Cross posthumously. The station was reduced to rubble but, had the whole train caught fire and exploded, Soham would have been virtually destroyed, with much loss of life.

Over on the other side of the world, in northern Australia, another wartime hero won glory of a different kind. On page 89 Ernestine Hill described her train journey across the Northern Territory. Many years later the little old engine called *Sentinel* was still working. The chief port of the Territory is Darwin and from it thousands of Australian and American troops embarked to fight the Japanese in the Second World War. The *Sentinel* was affectionately known to Australians as *Spirit of Protest*, and the troops readily adopted this name. Its story is told in J. H. and W. D. Martin's *The Australian Book of Trains*:

'Spirit of Protest' was dramatically jerked out of an easy, ambling, happy-go-lucky, get-there-some-day existence to undertake a task that would sour the boiler tubes of any self-respecting locomotive. It was bad enough to have to drag a huge train of camel trucks laden with noisy soldiers and equipment, and then dash back to haul a much too heavy load of supplies, but there was bombing to be dodged as well. For the entire war period the 'Spirit of Protest' took its corners with the utmost caution, because it never knew whether there would be any track just round the bend. After almost every raid a repair gang would be rushed to fill a crater and restore the line before her ladyship could pass. Sometimes soldiers were pressed into the job. Bank clerks, salesmen, journalists, cowhands, and a host of other fellows who thought a fishplate was something used in a restaurant, or ballast the stuff they put

in the bottom of ships, made a marvellous job of these quick and urgent repairs. It says much for their ingenuity and resourcefulness that they could signal that the line was all clear and safe for traffic long before the marauding bombers were back at their base.

It was a restless, relentless existence that the little locomotive endured. As well as dodging bombs and trundling between the two terminal points, it was often called upon to wander around the dock area or the meatworks to do a bit of spare-time shunting just to keep its hand in. Its arrival at Darwin was always hailed with delight, for it brought parcels from home, supplies, and, on memorable occasions, beer and tobacco. Its departure, on the other hand, was always watched with sadness and envy, for it invariably took sick and wounded men back to bases farther down the line.

The task was a twenty-four hour one, with no time for overhaul or complete repairs. It was a question of a quick patch-up on the job, and then back into the fray. If ever locomotives are decorated for meritorious service, then the 'Spirit of Protest' must surely have pride of place in the front row.

The United States has quite a folklore of railroad heroes, many of them celebrated in ballad, and sometimes in films. The following story occurred in September 1938, during one of the worst hurricanes to hit the east coast of the U.S.A. Harry Easton, driver, took his engine, the *Bostonian*, up the coast from New London to Boston, knowing full well that the hurricane was pursuing him, but trusting in his luck to get through before the worst happened. Louis Wolfe tells the story in *Clear the Track*:

Troops leaving Larrimah, central Australia, for the Northern Territory in 1944

After the train pulled past the town of Mystic, the hurricane hit with devilish fury. The wind walloped the side of the train like a mighty sledge-hammer. Easton slowed down to five miles an hour. He was taking no chances. The lives of almost three hundred passengers were in his hands.

One of the worst hurricanes in history was about to hit New England. Before it was over the sea would rise sixteen feet, the wind would blow at a speed of one hundred miles an hour. Millions of dollars worth of property would be destroyed, thousands of people would be made homeless, hundreds drowned or killed.

When the *Bostonian* neared Stonington station, Easton looked at the double track causeway that lay ahead. About 2,000 feet long, the causeway bridged a cove jutting in from Long Island Sound. Even now water lapped over the tracks and washed away part of the roadbed.

Slowly rolling his train onto the causeway, Easton gazed through the murky gloom to catch sight of the signal tower on the other side. But all he could see just then was telegraph wires strewn across the tracks, smashed rowboats, battered launches and other debris.

By the time the train was halfway across the causeway the tracks lay under water. The wind and rain battered the coaches. Easton prayed nothing would force him to stop on the causeway. But just then he sighted the signal-tower light ... it was red! Easton couldn't believe his eyes. He jammed on the brakes, and as the train groaned to a stop, he rasped, 'Man, alive! Of all the places to be stopped!'

Easton glanced back. The last four cars of the train were on banked tracks and leaning to one side. One powerful gust of wind and they would go over. The engineer yanked his whistle with all his might, calling for a green signal. But the wail of the whistle was swallowed up in the roar of the hurricane and the signal stayed red.

Easton climbed down from his engine and forged ahead through the windswept water and debris. Fifteen minutes later the engineer stood at the foot of the tower, cupped his hands and yelled, 'Hey, there. Hey, there.'

The towerman called down, 'What is it?'

'I can't stay out there all day. I've got three hundred passengers aboard. How about a go-head signal?'

'The signals are out of order,' the towerman yelled down. 'But go ahead anyway. Not too far. There's another train stalled up ahead.'

Easton turned and again plunged headlong into the storm. Now the water was waist high and rising fast. Again and again he slipped or was knocked down by the wreckage and powerful tide. But he staggered on.

But the instant Easton climbed into his cab, the conductor dashed up and gasped, 'The roadbed under the last four cars has been washed out.'

Easton paused for a moment. Then he snapped, 'Quick! Get the passengers into the forward cars. Then uncouple the last four cars and we'll pull out.'

When the scared passengers were ordered to crowd into the forward cars, they were on the verge of panic. Terror-stricken men and women shoved ahead like cattle. A mother and daughter plunged into the sea and swam for shore. A woman passenger and a dining car steward were drowned trying to swim to safety. Meanwhile, more wreckage became tightly wedged under the wheels of the cars up front. Now those could not be budged either.

'Move the passengers again,' Easton ordered, 'this time into the first car. Then uncouple that car from the rest of the train. Hurry!'

Again there was pushing and screaming. More passengers jumped into the sea. But in a short time the train crew huddled the remaining passengers into the first car and even up onto the engine.

Donoghue, a railroad man who happened to be a passenger, grappled with the coupling. The raging water washed over his head. Chunks of debris knocked him off his feet. But Donoghue stuck to the job and uncoupled the first car. Easton pulled the throttle back. The engine shuddered as it started plowing through the high water. As the train inched ahead a new danger cropped up. The fallen telegraph wires! Draped over the engine, they grew tighter with each turn of the wheels. One by one the telegraph poles toppled over with a crack.

With the wires and poles dragging along, Easton kept the engine plowing ahead. Rolling across the causeway, Easton spotted a wrecked cabin cruiser on the tracks. He slowed down almost to a stop, then expertly nudged the boat off to one side. A little while longer, Easton figured, and they all would be out of danger. But just then he saw the roof and top half of a house drifting toward the causeway. In the grip of the raging current, it drifted and then – came to a stop right on the tracks!

Easton slowly ran the engine right up to the house and stopped. He had no idea how heavy the house was, or how firmly wedged. Suppose he tried to push the house aside and the engine jumped the tracks ...

But there was no choice. Now the water was almost as high as the cab. Easton gripped the throttle and pulled back just a bit. Then the engine rolled ahead smack up against the side of the house. Easton added steam. There was a heavy crash and crunch. But the house did not budge. Easton added a little more steam. Now the engine was laboring. Easton pulled the throttle back further ... further ... then the house finally gave way. Only a little at first. But Easton expertly nudged the house off the tracks. A few minutes later he slumped down and relaxed for the first time in hours as he ran his one-coach train jammed with passengers up to Stonington station and safety.

For both the United States and Canada a railroad system was far more than a means of transport from one place to another. The railways that were built to span the North American continent were *politically* important. They acted as 'iron bonds' to hold

107

*A work gang on the
Canadian Pacific*

*An engineers' camp in
the Rockies during the
construction of the
Canadian Pacific*

A construction site near Rogers Pass, 1886

Left: a first-class carriage of the Canadian Pacific in 1895

Right: a 'colonist' or emigrant sleeping car, about 1884

together the States that made up these two huge North American countries.

Canada became a Dominion in 1867. It could not have existed without its two railroads, the Canadian Pacific and the Canadian National. Indeed the far-west province of British Columbia refused to join the new Dominion unless given a definite promise that a railroad would be built to unite her with the rest of Canada, and the east-coast States made the same demand. The railroads were the life-giving arteries of Canada, but they were to cost many lives before they were completed. The story of Walter Leamy, told in F. A. Talbot's *The Making of the Great Canadian Railway*, is an example of the quiet heroism of the men who built the Canadian Pacific Railway across 3,000 miles and played a part in the fight through the Rocky Mountains to the west coast.

The cemeteries around Ottawa, and at a dozen other places up and down the country, can give grim and tragic evidence of this fight. The brief epitaphs relate how those beneath the soil met their end in some unfortunate manner while searching for the easy grade. Even the woods mourn over some hero who is sleeping the long sleep beneath a rough mound, carefully railed in with a picket fence and marked with a rude wooden cross. If one searches the pay-rolls, one will find here and there the record of a man who set out bravely into the woods never more to be seen or heard of again. The forests and the rivers guard their secrets tightly.

Every day some daring deed was accomplished; every hour could relate some display of sacrifice; every mile of the line commemorates the heroism of a score of rough-and-ready boys of the bush. There was Walter Leamy. He was in charge of a transport party, and had a large bulk of supplies which it was imperative should be got through. He was working on one of the most difficult sections at the time, and the winter was one of terrible severity. The party were painfully making their arduous way forward through soft snow and a blinding blizzard. At last they ran into a bad stretch of snow, which compelled a halt for deliberation. One of the men volunteered to push ahead to reconnoitre, but Leamy, being the officer-in-charge, refused to entertain the proposal. It was his duty to pilot the party through, and if any risks were to be run, it was his place to incur them. So he started off, promising to return without delay the moment he found a practical solution of the difficulty.

But the rest of the party waited in vain. The hours slipped by without bringing any signs of the transport officer's return. The worst was feared, so the party thereupon moved forward warily. Their leader's tracks were plainly visible in the snow, and they dogged them step by step. In due course they came to the edge of the narrows of Opasatica

Lake, and the imprints went still onward over its icebound surface. But the boldest among the party did not like the outlook. That lake was covered with slush, and this is far more treacherous than quicksand. The cause of the leader's non-return was revealed as plainly as an open book. He had pushed on speedily, had gained the edge of the lake, and without pausing, had ventured on its dangerous surface. The ice had collapsed under his weight, and the icy shell had closed over him.

The men of the forest had reconstructed the tragedy only too vividly. When the ice broke the lake gave up the body of the heroic transport officer, and it now lies sleeping in the cemetery of Hull, within sight of the office whence he received his commission.

The United States started to build its railroads almost as early as

Kate Shelley, shown here twenty-five years after her heroic action

Britain. By 1840, 2,818 miles of track were open, and by 1860,
30,000 miles. The immense expansion of railroad-building in the
eighties brought this total up to 193,000 miles. It is to this period
that one of America's most exciting stories of railroad heroism
belongs, the story of Kate Shelley. She was one of five children
born to Irish immigrant parents who lived in a shack at Honey
Creek, near Boone, in Iowa, a mile and a half from a sizeable river
called the Des Moines. The shack commanded a view of the bridge
over the creek that carried the Chicago and North-west main line,
on which Kate's father had worked till his death. Kate was the eldest
of the five orphaned children, a short, stocky girl, deeply religious
and hard-working. The account of her heroism, at the age of fifteen,
was contributed mainly by her brother, who was only six at the
time but remembered it vividly. It is told in F. H. Hubbard's
Railroad Avenue:

As darkness fell with thunder claps and lightning glare in the later
afternoon of July 6th, 1881, the widow Shelley and her brood huddled
together in their home, gazing out anxiously at the black clouds and the
rain. The river was to rise six inches within an hour, and before morning eleven of the twenty-one bridges in the Moines Valley would be
swept away by flood. Night deepened. The young children dozed fitfully,
but Kate and her mother watched and waited. Honey Creek was edging
higher and higher. It carried on its frothy bosom bits of flotsam that
lightning flashes revealed as fence posts, boards and uprooted trees.

Shortly after eleven o'clock Kate and her mother heard a train rumble
onto the creek bridge, and discerned through the rainy blackness the
stab of a headlight beam. (This was in fact only an engine, with four
men on the footplate.)

Kate saw the engine begin to cross Honey Creek bridge that was now
swaying crazily, and distinctly heard the engine bell toll once, twice, and
then –

'Oh, mother!' she screamed, 'they've gone down!'

It was true. A terrific crash and gurgle and the hiss of escaping steam
arose above the wail of wind-driven rain. Kate realized that she must go to
the help of the men, and stop the passenger train that would soon be
due at Moingona, the midnight train from the west. With her mother's
blessing, she set out, carrying an old lantern, with a piece of felt skirt
for a wick. Finding that the deluge had risen far above all paths and
roadways, the girl realized that she could not walk the track to reach
the collapsed bridge, so she climbed the bluff at the rear of the cabin
and made a curving detour to the bridge.

Reaching the scene of disaster, she saw that part of the bridge still
remained. She swung her feeble lantern and shouted as loudly as she

could. A faint answer came from below from the engineer, Ed Wood, and his brakeman, Agar. She distinguished them by jagged lightning that ripped the sky for a brief instant. The two men had escaped drowning by clinging to some driftwood and drawing themselves above the swollen creek onto overhanging trees, but their two companions were missing.

The midnight limited, as it was called, was almost due. Moingona was only a mile away, but between her and the village lay the sullen Des Moines River, which was now so gorged that it almost lapped the ties on the long, wooden railroad bridge.

Kate had long since been drenched to the skin. She tried to think clearly. The only route to Moingona lay across that bridge, at the risk of death to herself, but if she did not get there and in time, that trainload of human beings was doomed. But what if the express should catch her on the bridge, and roll past in the darkness, onto the broken Honey Creek span and down into the turbulent stream, the coaches filling with water? These fears tortured the girl as she buffeted the wind and rain, her strength drained away, and stood at last on the river's bank.

The gale extinguished her dim light. She stumbled and slipped her way from one tie to the next. She did not run, she did not even walk. She *crawled*. On hands and knees she fought physical and mental terrors as she pushed ahead to the far side of the bridge, groping through darkness, her lips trembling in prayer. From time to time her skirt became entangled in spikes, toppling her off balance. Other spikes and splinters cut and bruised her hands and knees. Every moment she was fearful of seeing the headlight of the east bound limited shine full on her face.

The old lantern that Kate Shelley carried with her

Moingona depot, the station into which Kate Shelley staggered after her incredible journey

Panic gripped Kate when, about halfway across, she saw a huge tree, its roots thickly matted with earth clods, bearing down upon her like a giant battering-ram. But somehow it passed harmlessly between the piers [of the bridge] spraying her with leaves and spume, and she continued to creep toward the end of the bridge which appeared so very far away. Finally ... she stood on solid embankment and paused a moment to catch her strangled breath. Then she attempted to run at top speed to the Moingona depot, half a mile away. She never could recall afterward, how she tottered into the station, wild-eyed, hatless and disheveled, and gasped her message.

The few almost inarticulate words she uttered were enough for the agent. Grabbing a red lantern, he dashed outside just as an engine whistle announced that the express was rolling through. His frantic signal brought the train grinding to a halt. The engineer descended from his cab, ready to bawl out the agent for stopping the hotshot at a small way station, and on such a night. The conductor swung off, too; and soon the passengers piled out of the cars.

The girl gave vent to a torrent of words. Its effect on her listeners was electrifying. Men cheered, women wept; several persons flung their arms around the young heroine and kissed her.

But Kate had not forgotten Engineer Wood and Brakeman Agar clinging to a precarious perch on the flood-ridden bank of Honey Creek.

A rescue party brought them both back to safety. Section Foreman Donahue's dead body was found in a cornfield. Foreman Olmstead's body was never found. Kate Shelley was showered with gifts, and a new iron bridge over the Des Moines River was named after her. In 1903 she became the station agent at Moingona, and on 12 January 1912 she died. In 1933 the track that passed the Shelley cottage was ripped up. One of the ballads about her ends:

The Kate Shelley Bridge over the Des Moines River

Nine and forty years are gone; the trains no longer come
Along the crest of Honey Creek before Kate Shelley's home.
Oh, there were songs for other years when all the road was hers—
And there were men to bless her name, and gold to fill her purse.

But if you go to Honey Creek in some dark summer storm,
Be sure you take a lantern flame to keep your spirit warm.
For there will be a phantom train, and foggy whistle cries—
And in the lightning flare you'll see Kate Shelley on the ties.

Kate Shelley in later life when she had become station agent at Moingona

Buffer: Casey Jones

Come all you rounders, if you want to hear
Story about a brave ingineer.

Now, 'K.C.' *Jones* was this rounder's *name*,
On a six-eight-wheeler, boys, he won his fame.
Caller called K.C. at a half-past *four*,
Kissed his wife at the station *door*,
Mounted to the cabin with his orders in his hand,
Took his farewell trip to the Promised Land.

> *Casey Jones! Mounted to the cabin,*
> *Casey Jones! with his orders in his hand.*
> *Casey Jones! Mounted to the cabin,*
> *Took his farewell trip to the Promised Land.*

'Put *in* yo' water, an' ashovel in yo' *coal*,
Stick yo' head *out* the winda, watch them drivers *roll*,
I'll *run* her *till* she *leaves* the rail,
'Cause I'm eight hours *late* with that western mail.'
Looked *at* his *watch*, an' his watch was *slow*;
Looked *at* the water, an' the *water* was low.
Turned to the fireman, an' then he *said*,
'We're gonna reach Frisco, but we'll all be dead.'

> *Casey Jones! Gonna reach Frisco,*
> *Casey Jones! but we'll all be dead.*
> *Casey Jones! Gonna reach Frisco,*
> *Gonna reach Frisco, but we'll all be dead.*

K.C. pulled *up* that Remo *hill*,
Whistled for the crossin' with an *awful* shrill.
Switchman *knew* by the ingine's *moans*
That the man *at* the throttle *was* K.C. *Jones*.
Pulled up within two *miles* of the place
Number *Four starin'* him right in the face!
Turned to the fireman says, 'Boy, better *jump*,
'Cause there's *two* locomotives that's a-gointa *bump*.'

> *Casey Jones! Two locomotives,*
> *Casey Jones! that's a-gointa bump,*
> *Casey Jones! Two locomotives,*
> *Two locomotives that's a-gointa bump.*

Casey Jones's whistle

Casey Jones's fireman,
Sim Webb

K.C. *said* jes' befo' he *died*,
'*Two mo*' roads, that I wanted to ride.'
Fireman says 'What *can* they be?'
'It's the Southern Pa*ci*fic, and the Santa Fe.'
Missis *Jones* sat *on* her *bed*, a sighin',
Jes' received a message that K.C. was dyin',
Says, '*Go* to bed, chillun, an' *hush* yo' cryin',
'Cause you got another poppa on the Salt Lake Line.'

Missis Casey Jones! Got another poppa,
Missis Casey Jones! on the Salt Lake Line.
Missis Casey Jones! Got another poppa,
Got another poppa on the Salt Lake Line.

Anon.

John Luther Jones
(1864–1900) took the
name Casey from his
boyhood town of Cayce,
Kentucky

The engine that Casey
Jones drove

Chapter Eight

Railway crime

Trains have been used as scenes for crime by several well-known thriller-writers, among them Agatha Christie in her *Murder on the Orient Express*. In reality railways *have* often enough been in the news in connection with some crime, among the commonest being robbery. Trains carry valuable freight such as gold bullion, bank notes and registered mail – obvious targets for thieves.

One of the earliest railway robberies, in 1844, gave an astonished public (and an equally astonished and confounded criminal world)

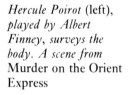

Hercule Poirot (left), *played by Albert Finney, surveys the body. A scene from* Murder on the Orient Express

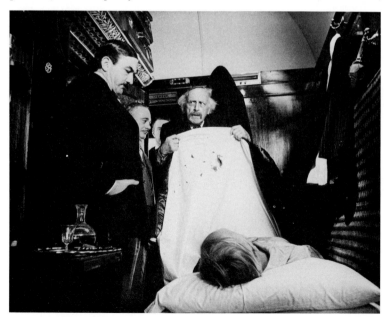

news of a brand-new device, the 'electric constable', that is, the electric telegraph system, for the first time used to catch some train thieves. This account is by Kellow Chesney in *The Victorian Underworld*.

The Commissioners of Police having issued orders that several officers of the detective force shall be stationed at Paddington to watch the movements of suspicious persons, going by the down train, and give notice by the electric telegraph to the Slough Station of the number of such suspected persons, and dress, their names (if known), also the carriages in which they are.

Now come the messages following one after the other, and influencing the fate of the marked individuals with all the celerity, certainty and calmness of the Nemesis of Greek drama:

Paddington, 10.20 a.m. – Mail train just started. It contains three thieves, named Sparrow, Burrell and Spurgeon, in the first compartment of the fourth first-class carriage.

Slough, 10.50 a.m. – Mail train arrived. The officers have cautioned the three thieves.

Paddington, 10.50 a.m. – Special train just left. It contained two thieves; one named Owen Martin, who is dressed in black, *crape on his hat*; the other named Fiddler Dick, in black trousers and light blouse. Both in the third compartment of the first second-class carriage.

Slough, 11.16 a.m. – Special train arrived. Officers have taken the two thieves into custody, a lady having lost her bag, containing a purse with two sovereigns and some silver in it; one of the sovereigns was sworn to by the lady as having been her property. It was found in Fiddler Dick's watch fob.

It appears that, on the arrival of the train, a policeman opened the door of the 'third compartment of the first second-class carriage', and asked the passengers if they had missed anything? A search in pockets and bags accordingly ensued, until one lady called out that her purse was gone.

'Fiddler Dick, you are wanted,' was the immediate demand of the police officer, beckoning to the culprit, who came out of the carriage thunderstruck at the discovery, and gave himself up, together with the booty, with the air of a completely beaten man.

The story of Charlie Peace, murderer and burglar, filled the newspapers of 1879, and his attempt, when captured, to escape from a train caught public imagination. Here is an account of it by John Pendleton, a devotee of railways, who regaled his readers with a rich crop of anecdotes in a two-volume work called *Our Railways*, published in 1894:

The murderer and burglar, who was one of the most startling

The spot at Darnall near Worksop where Charlie Peace (inset) *escaped from the train and was later recaptured*

products of modern society, was taken, on January 22, 1879 – after his capture by Sergeant Robinson on the lawn in St John's Park, Blackheath – by train on his way to Sheffield, where he was to undergo examination before the magistrates for the murder of Arthur Dyson, civil engineer, at Banner Cross.

The notoriety of the criminal had become almost the country's talk. His resource and daring were almost on everybody's tongue. 'It would be a funny thing if he escaped,' said a spectator, chatting to an official in the Sheffield Police Court, which was crammed with a crowd, waiting in eager expectation for the prisoner's arrival. Scarcely were the words uttered than there was an indescribable flutter in the Court, much whispering, and many serious faces. Charles Peace had escaped! All the way down from Pentonville the man, who was restless, savage, and snarling, just like a wild beast, gave the warders continual trouble. When the Great Northern express was speeding through the pastoral country a little north of Worksop, Peace, jibing and sneering at his jailers, sprang to the carriage window and took a flying leap out of the express. But his panther-like action availed him little. The under-warder seized him by the left foot as he leapt from the compartment, and held on with desperate grasp. The other warder tugged at the communication-cord, but it would not act.

On went the express by field and homestead, the driver unaware of the fierce struggle behind. Peace, suspended head downward, with his face banging now and then against the oscillating carriage, tried with his right leg to kick himself free from the warder's grip. The struggling attracted the attention of the passengers, but they could do nothing to assist the warder, who, with every muscle quivering, was straining with his writhing prisoner. Shout after shout passed from carriage to carriage, only to be carried miles away by the wind. The noise of the clamouring travellers simply made strange echoes in the driver's ears. For two miles the struggle went on. Then Peace, determined to end it, whatever the result to himself, wriggled his left foot out of his shoe, which was left in the warder's grasp, and at last he was free. He fell wildly, his head struck the carriage footboard with tremendous force, and he bounded into the six-foot, where he rolled over and over, a curious bundle half enveloped in a cloud of dust.

Still onward sped the train, the warder, helpless to secure his prey, craning his neck as far as he could out of the carriage window, his face a study of rage and concern because he had been outwitted. Nearly another mile was covered before the express pulled up. No time was then lost in chasing the fugitive. The warders, accompanied by several passengers eager for adventure, ran back along the line and found Peace in the six-foot not far from the place at which he had made his reckless descent from the train. The man was lying near the down track, a huddled heap, unconscious, with a serious wound in his head. He was not merely a person of amazing unscrupulousness, but of wondrous vitality, and he soon recovered sensibility, murmuring, as he was lifted into the guard's van of a goods train for removal to Sheffield, 'I am cold; cover me up.' The warders were only too pleased to cover him up; they took every care of him. When he was conveyed to Armley in readiness for his trial they were armed with revolvers; but the 'small, elderly-looking, feeble man, in brown convict-dress', made no further attempt to escape. He was sentenced to death at Leeds Assizes and hanged, no one regretting the hardened criminal's doom.

The railway Companies have always employed their own policemen. Sometimes their work brings them into great danger. As long ago as 1895 a policeman, Detective Sergeant Kidd, was killed on duty, and this incident is described by J. R. Whitbread in *The Railway Policeman*. With a colleague called Osborne, he spent some months at Wigan, patrolling the station for thieves.

One Sunday evening after dark the two detectives set out to patrol the sidings. With the moon nearly full, they could see a long way across the yard. As they came round a wall they saw in a patch of clear light a man crouching on the ground and looking over towards a line of waggons. Osborne rushed after the man, who immediately took to his heels, but the detective managed to pin him against a goods-van. They grappled and rolled on the ground, while Robert Kidd dashed around behind the waggons.

Osborne was having a rough time with his man and suddenly two others tackled him. He got onto his feet and flailed about him with his truncheon to such good effect that the two newcomers broke and fled.

Then he returned to the struggle with the first man. But there he was not so successful, and the man overwhelmed him, half stunned him with his own truncheon, and escaped.

Osborne was in a daze as he went in search of his fellow-officer. He found Kidd slumped on his hands and knees beside the railway track with blood streaming down his face. Osborne was on the point of collapse himself, and remembered little more until he awoke in hospital. Then he learned that somehow he had managed to reach the nearest signal-box and get the help of some railwaymen.

Sergeant Kidd had been carried to the passenger station, but was dead before a doctor could be brought. He had been slashed and stabbed nine times about the face, head, and neck, so that two main arteries had been severed. There were other stab wounds upon his arms, and the tip of one finger had been sliced off.

A search of the sidings confirmed that there had been a desperate struggle against odds during that ten minutes, and two bloodstained caps were found close by a waggon whose cover had been cut open. Kidd's handcuffs lay in a pool of his blood.

The first of the three men was in the hands of the police in less than six hours after the murder, thanks to information received around two public houses in Wigan. He was William Kearsley, a collier, and Osborne readily identified him ...

In the next two days the others were rounded up, one of them, William Halliwell, having slept out in a boat on the canal. This man, who was the one with whom Detective Osborne had had the unsuccessful tussle, was prepared to give evidence against his two accomplices, the third of whom turned out to be another collier, Elijah Winstanley, a half-brother of Kearsley.

All three were charged with the wilful murder of Sergeant Kidd, and when the case came before the Wigan Borough Police Court, Winstanley became hysterical in the dock and started to shout, 'Kill me. Kill me. Go on it's murder – I did it. I didn't intend killing him.' He and Kearsley were both committed for trial for murder, and Halliwell on the lesser charge of unlawful wounding ...

The case attracted a great deal of attention when the trial at last took place at Liverpool Assizes. In the interval the murder weapon, a penknife with a notch on one blade, had been found by a group of workmen playing cards in a field less than a hundred yards from where Sergeant Kidd had fought for his life ...

The jury reached its verdict without leaving the court, finding Winstanley and Kearsley guilty. Both were sentenced to death. Halliwell ... was discharged.

Winstanley, who had declared that he and not Kearsley had killed the sergeant, was executed, but Kearsley received a reprieve and had his sentence commuted to penal servitude ...

Afterwards the people of Wigan started to raise funds for the families of Winstanley and Kearsley, and the Wigan brass band played through the main streets to collect contributions.

It was left to the Mayor of Salford to open an appeal for the widow of Sergeant Kidd, who was struggling to raise seven young children completely unprovided for.

And what caused the death of one brave man and the death of his craven killer? Men often commit murder for gold, but in this tragic case the rifled goods-van had held only a consignment of sweets.

The most famous crime on the lines was the Great Mail Robbery of 1963. Interestingly a very similar crime was committed over a hundred years earlier. Compared with the 1963 robbery it may seem insignificant, involving a mere £12,000 worth of bullion as against nearly £3 million worth of bank-notes, but it caused a tremendous furore at the time and, although by 1963 criminals had become far more sophisticated in their methods, security, as you will see, does not seem to have improved much in the hundred-odd years between 1855 and 1963.

The 1855 story is told in *The Victorian Underworld*.

Perhaps the most sensational theft of the mid-century was the removal of £12,000 in gold coin and ingots from a train. Round the time of the Crimean War, shipments of gold from London to Paris were regular enough to attract the attention of criminals and allow careful plans to be laid, and this particular gang took full advantage of the opportunities. So far as was ever revealed, the prime mover was a man called Pierce. He had a criminal record and had been employed in a betting shop – a common hang-out for disreputable characters. Pierce brought into the scheme two vital accomplices; a clerk in the Southern Eastern Railway's traffic department by the name of Tester and a skilled screwsman, Agar. There must also have been other helping hands, perhaps unaware of the full scope of the plan.

The routine with the bullion was to pack each consignment in sealed iron-bound boxes which were placed inside steel safes. These were loaded on a London–Folkestone passenger train and at Folkestone harbour transferred to the Boulogne steam packet. The railway officials, who were responsible for the gold in transit, evidently felt such confidence in the heavy modern safes that no other special precautions were taken; the consignments travelled in the guard's custody in his van with other luggage. (The guard did not, of course, leave his van while the train was moving.) The safes had similar double locks and needed two keys to open them; and there were two sets of these keys in the railway company's possession, one with the traffic superintendent in London, the other at Folkestone.

The conspirators spent more than a year preparing for the big pull, during which time they achieved two essential and tricky objectives. They succeeded in corrupting a guard called Burgess who was sometimes employed on the run; and they got duplicates of the safe keys. Tester, the traffic clerk, was able to get hold of a single key for long enough to show it to Agar who took a wax impression. Then slackness at the traffic department at Folkestone provided another opportunity. Pierce, who had been keeping the place under observation and was lurking ready, found a moment when there was no clerk in the office and slipped in. There, in an unlocked cupboard, was the key they wanted, and he was able to remove it, get another quick impression taken by Agar, and put it back in its place without anyone apparently being the wiser.

All was now ready.

One day in May 1855 Agar and Pierce, equipped with several couriers' bags, took first-class tickets to Folkestone. The porters who put the bags in the guard's van must have found them particularly heavy for their size, as they contained a large quantity of small-shot sewn in pockets. Pierce took a seat in a carriage but Agar, waiting till the train was just moving out, hopped into the van at the end of the train, an action that evidently excited no particular notice. Their information was correct; Burgess was in charge and three safes on board. Agar unlocked one, carefully opened a bullion box, removed the gold, substituted lead shot, refastened and resealed the box, locked up the safe again and put the gold in his courier bag in place of the lead. At Redhill Tester met the train and collected the bag with the gold, while Pierce walked down the platform and managed to join Agar in the van. During the rest of the journey they took part of the contents of the other two safes, substituting lead, resealing and relocking as before. At Folkestone, while the safes were being unloaded, they hid in a dark corner of the van; then when all was clear they got out with their heavy bags. Instead of returning direct to London they went first to Dover. They had previously got hold of tickets for the Ostend–Dover crossing, and gave the impression of being travellers from the Continent.

The theft was not discovered until the safes were eventually opened in France, when a discrepancy was noticed in the weight of a box. Reports of the case roused great excitement: the substitution of the lead, the sealed bullion boxes and the locked, undamaged safes made a dramatic newspaper story, and of course immediately directed attention to the officials responsible for packing up the gold in the first place. It was not until after endless inquiry and many abortive arrests that, eighteen months later, the authorities got a firm line. And then, seemingly, it was only through a stroke of luck. Agar was arrested over an affair involving a cheque forgery. He had a mistress by whom he had had a child, and now,

in a desperate situation, he wanted her to be given some money from his share of the proceeds of the train robbery. But Pierce, who was actually holding the funds, seems to have decided either that this was a good opportunity to cheat his partner or that it would be dangerous to let the woman handle the money. Either way, his reluctance to disgorge had fatal results. Agar's woman knew something about how the robbery had been carried out, and when she was convinced that Pierce meant to cheat her, she turned informer. Agar, in Newgate and facing transportation, followed suit. Pierce, Tester and Burgess were all caught and sentenced, on Agar's evidence, to long terms.

The Great Mail Robbery of 1963 took place at about 3.10 a.m. on 8 August, when a gang of men ambushed a twelve-coach mail train bound for London from Glasgow. The robbers tampered with a signal just south of Leighton Buzzard – they stuffed a glove into the green light and lit up the red by putting electric batteries behind it – and the driver of the mail train, of course, stopped the train. His assistant alighted from the car to phone the signal box, but found the wires cut. On returning to the train, he was set upon and pushed back up into the cab where the driver had been coshed. Members of the gang then handcuffed them together. Meanwhile the two front coaches had been uncoupled (these were the ones containing the most valuable registered parcels), and the train was moved off down the track several hundred yards to where a white marker had been placed. Other members of the gang smashed into the two coaches and tossed the mail bags down the embankment to a waiting lorry.

Jack Mills, the driver
of the mail train

The story is taken up by Roy Perrott, writing in the *Observer*, 29 March 1964:

From the gang's point of view, everything depended on how much time they could allow themselves before the alarm was raised. A detailed knowledge of railway working was vital since – once the driver and fireman were handcuffed and rendered ineffective – a great deal hung on the guard's likely speed of action.

126

Timetable for success

The success of the plan required that for a vital period the guard and the train's 70 post office sorters would remain unalarmed in the 10 uncoupled rear coaches of the train while the gang unloaded two tons of paper money from the 'high value' coaches – conveniently hauled a quarter mile forward to a bridge over the road and the waiting getaway vehicles.

The gang had cut the telephone wires alongside the track and to the farmhouse near by. So, with knowledge of railway procedure, they could fairly confidently predict that their time allowance for the job went something like this:

1. Train halted 3.5 a.m. Uncoupling of train registered on indicator in guard's van. Guard, following rule book (and, of course, not suspecting nature of emergency) walks quickly back along the track for three quarters of a mile, placing detonators on line at quarter-mile intervals to protect mail train from other traffic; then returns to sorting vans (allow him 40 minutes, say, to assess situation and cover the distance).
2. Guard sees nothing of footplate crew, so walks forward 400 yards to halted engine at Bridego Bridge and finds handcuffed footplate crew (say 10 minutes).
3. Guard runs and walks at best middle-aged speed to nearest telephone at Cheddington signal-box, one and a half miles distant (20 minutes).

The gang worked fast, in a well-drilled silence, at the job of uncoupling the train, moving the cash-coaches forward, unloading 120 mail bags and stowing them in the lorry. It took them 40 minutes and even at that they were evidently running on the very edge of their schedule, if not over it.

They left the scene at 3.45 a.m. From their long observation of the line they knew that a goods train was due to pass in a few minutes.

Leaving the driver and his assistant in the train, the robbers made their getaway in waiting cars. They had nearly an hour's start on the police.

Detective Superintendent Malcolm Fewtrell, head of Buckinghamshire C.I.D., has described how the police set about finding the thieves:

We searched the carriages but there were no fingerprints or clues of any sort. We worked out the staggering sum that had been stolen – £2,600,000. Strangely they left behind £40,000. Whether this was because they were working to a tight deadline, or were tired from lifting the sacks of money, we never found out.

The nearest main road to the abandoned train was the M1 and at first we automatically assumed that the money had gone straight to London, but quite quickly we received some good information that the gang had a hideout not too far from the bridge. I asked the Press to help and it was largely due to their cooperation in giving us so much publicity that a

A view of Leatherslade Farm, showing a lorry and two Land-Rovers used by the gang to take the money from the train to the hideout

A view of Leatherslade Farm, showing a lorry and two Land-Rovers used by the gang to take the money from the train to the hideout

cowman, John Maris, came forward and mentioned Leatherslade Farm – that was the following Tuesday, 13 August.

When we arrived the whole inquiry changed dramatically as the place was one big clue. We found a lorry, three cars, mail bags containing empty money wrappers, and best of all loads of fingerprints. We dusted everything from the eggs to the lorry and later at the court it was on fingerprint evidence that all the men, except Goody, were convicted. The cowman received £18,000 reward money.

The trial, which began on 20 January 1964, was like a thriller in the way it unfolded. Because of the world-wide interest in the case there wasn't a local court big enough and we borrowed the Urban District Council offices in Aylesbury. But the place lacked security. We knew that several of the accused would be rather anxious to leave, so we borrowed a mobile prison van which contained small cells about 2 ft by 4 ft, and the accused were taken from Aylesbury prison to the court in the morning, back to prison for lunch, back to the court after lunch and back to prison in the evening.

In the periodical *New Society*, on 22 August 1963, Colin Mac-Innes added a comment about the Great Mail Robbery under the title 'Kelly rides again':

There is also something so *comical* about a train containing a vast fortune that is provided with no guard whatever, that the crime cannot be taken as seriously as it might be. By 1963, security precautions, both material and human, have reached an extraordinary degree of complexity in any place where valuables are secreted. But to send this Ali Baba's cave of treasure hurtling down the main line without so much as an old age pensioner to keep a look out, has such an element of the improbable as to render its subsequent fate a little ludicrous.

And there is the gang... The fiddling with the signals, the uncoupling of the carriages, the cheeky driving on of the train to a convenient destination, the 15 minutes it all took, the rapid disappearance into the night: The very fact that a train was treated with such levity adds to the fascination. For everyone has dreamed, at one time or another, of taking liberties with something so majestic as a night express.

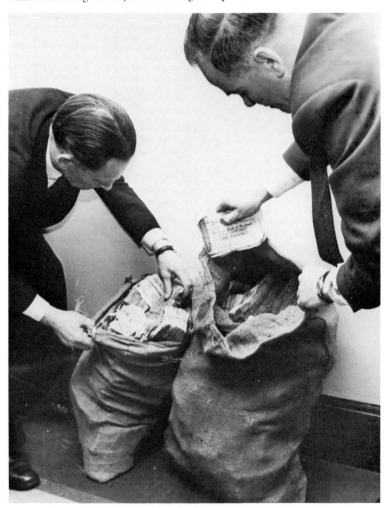

Two dirty potato sacks containing about £50,000 of stolen money were found in a telephone box four months after the robbery

Buffer : Night mail

This is the night mail crossing the border,
Bringing the cheque and the postal order,
Letters for the rich, letters for the poor,
The shop at the corner and the girl next door,
Pulling up Beattock, a steady climb—
The gradient's against her but she's on time.

Past cotton grass and moorland boulder,
Shovelling white steam over her shoulder,
Snorting noisily as she passes
Silent miles of wind-bent grasses;

Birds turn their heads as she approaches,
Stare from the bushes at her blank-faced coaches;
Sheepdogs cannot turn her course
They slumber on with paws across,
In the farm she passes no one wakes,
But a jug in a bedroom gently shakes.

Dawn freshens, the climb is done.
Down towards Glasgow she descends
Towards the steam tugs, yelping down the glade of cranes
Towards the fields of apparatus, the furnaces
Set on the dark plain like gigantic chessmen,
All Scotland waits for her;
In the dark glens, beside the pale-green sea lochs,
Men long for news.

Letters of thanks, letters from banks,
Letters of joy from the girl and boy,
Receipted bills and circulations
To inspect new stock or visit relations,
And applications for situations,
And timid lovers' declarations,
And gossip, gossip from all the nations,
News circumstantial, news financial,
Letters with holiday snaps to enlarge in,
Letters with faces scrawled in the margin,
Letters from uncles, cousins and aunts,
Letters to Scotland from the South of France,
Letters of condolence to Highlands and Lowlands,
Notes from overseas to the Hebrides;
Written on paper of every hue,
The pink, the violet, the white and the blue,
The chatty, the catty, the boring, adoring,

The cold and official and the heart's outpouring,
Clever, stupid, short and long,
The typed and the printed and the spelt all wrong,
Thousands are still asleep
Dreaming of terrifying monsters
Or a friendly tea beside the band at Cranston's or Crawford's;
Asleep in working Glasgow, asleep in well-set Edinburgh,
Asleep in granite Aberdeen.
They continue their dreams
But shall wake soon and long for letters,
And none will hear the postman's knock
Without a quickening of the heart,
For who can bear to feel himself forgotten?

W. H. AUDEN

Railway facts and feats

Railways

Britain The first public goods railway in the world was sanctioned by Parliament on 21 May 1801. It was the Surrey Iron Railway.

The first railway to carry fare-paying passengers was the Oystermouth Railway, near Swansea. It opened in 1806, using horse traction, and celebrated 150 years of passenger services in 1956, having changed first to steam, then electricity, then petrol, then diesel. It was dismantled in 1960.

The first public railway to use steam from the start was the Stockton and Darlington Railway, which opened on 27 September 1825.

America The first American steam locomotive was built in 1825.

The first regular steam railroad was the South Carolina Railroad, which opened on 15 January 1831.

The first Canadian steam railway was the Champlain and St Lawrence Railway, which opened on 21 July 1836, using a locomotive, the *Dorchester*, built by Robert Stephenson's firm.

Australia The first steam-operated railway was the Melbourne and Hobson's Bay Railway, 2·5 miles long.

An early engine used on the Champlain and St Lawrence Railway

Railway track

British Rail consumes about 2,500,000 sleepers or ties annually. The number of sleepers *per mile* varies from 2,112 to 2,464.

The longest *straight* stretch of track in the world is on the Transcontinental Railway in Australia – 297 miles.

The longest railway in the world is the Trans-Siberian Railway from Moscow to Vladivostock – 5,801 miles. The Trans-Siberian Express covers the journey in nine days, three hours.

A stretch of the Transcontinental Railway, Australia

The Trans-Siberian Express

134

Bridges and tunnels

The world's longest railway bridge is the Huey P. Long Bridge, New Orleans – 4 miles, 705 yards.

Europe's longest is the Tay Bridge, Scotland – 2 miles, 1,093 yards.

The first underwater railway tunnel was the Thames Tunnel, built by Brunel's father, Marc Brunel, in 1825. It is now part of London Transport.

The longest tunnel in the world is the Severn Tunnel, on the old Great Western Railway – 4 miles, 628 yards.

The Tay Bridge

Sir Marc Brunel is welcomed to the Thames Tunnel banquet by his son

135

Speed records

The world speed record for a steam locomotive was achieved by
the L.N.E.R. engine *Mallard*, on 3 July 1938, when *Mallard*
reached 126 m.p.h. descending Stoke Bank. The engine is preserved
at the National Railway Museum, York.

   The world's present rail speed record was achieved in France, on
4 December 1967, with a speed of 235 m.p.h. reached by *l' Aérotrain*,
powered by jet aero engines

The Mallard

L'Aérotrain

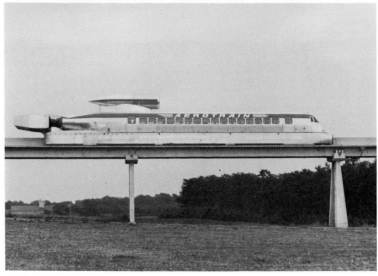

Miscellaneous

The first recorded rail accident was the death of William Huskisson, M.P., run over by Stephenson's *Rocket* on 15 September 1830.

The worst rail disaster occured in Spain in 1944, when a train was wrecked in a tunnel, with 500–800 people killed.

The world's largest railway station is the Grand Central Terminal, New York, with 44 platforms, about 550 trains a day, carrying 180,000 people.

The world's highest railway station is Ticlio, on the Central Railway of Peru, which was opened in 1904 and stands 15,610 feet up in the mountains.

The station with the longest name was in Anglesey, North Wales, but was closed in 1972. It was called:

Llanfairpwllgwyngillgogerychwyrndrobwllllantysiliogogogoch.

This means 'Mary's church by the white hazel pool near the fierce whirlpool with the church of Tysilio by the red cave'.

The first underground passenger railway in the world was the Metropolitan Railway of London, opened in 1863.

Left: *the forecourt of Grand Central, New York*

Above: *Baker Street, one of the stations on the Metropolitan line*

Book list

CASSERLEY, H. C., *Railways Since 1939*, David & Charles, 1972; *Railways Between the Wars*, David & Charles, 1971.

COLEMAN, Terry, *Railway Navvies: A History of the Men Who Made Railways*, Hutchinson, 1965/Penguin, 1970.

DAVIES, H., *George Stephenson*, Weidenfeld & Nicolson, 1975.

HUBBARD, Freeman H., *Railroad Avenue*, McGraw-Hill, 1945.

JONES, Kenneth Westcott, *Romantic Railways*, Arlington Books, 1971.

LEGG, Stuart, ed., *The Railway Book*, Hart-Davis, 1952.

McKILLOP, Norman, *Western Rail Trail*, Nelson, 1962.

MARSHALL, John, *The Guinness Book of Rail Facts and Feats*, Guinness Superlatives, 1976 (2nd edition).

MARTIN, J. H. and W. D., *The Australian Book of Trains*, Angus & Robertson, 1947.

MORGAN, B., ed., *The Great Trains*, Patrick Stephens Ltd, 1973.

NOCK, O. S., *British Trains Past and Present*, Batsford, 1951; *Continental Main Lines, Today and Yesterday*, Allen & Unwin, 1963; *The Father of Railways: The Story of George Stephenson*, Nelson, 1958; *Historic Railway Disasters*, Ian Allan, 1969/Arrow, 1970; *Railways of Australia*, A. & C. Black, 1971; *Railways of Canada*, A. & C. Black, 1973.

REYNOLDS, M., *Engine-driving Life*, 1881.

ROBBINS, M., *The Railway Age*, Penguin, 1970.

ROLT, L. T. C., *Isambard Kingdom Brunel*, Longman, 1957/Penguin, 1970; *Red for Danger*, David & Charles, 1971/Pan, 1971.

SIMMONS, Jack, *Railways of Britain*, Macmillan, 1968.

Index